THE
EXPERIENCE
OF CHRIST

WITNESS LEE

Living Stream Ministry
Anaheim, California

© 1978 Living Stream Ministry

All rights reserved. No part of this work may be reproduced or transmitted in any form or by any means—graphic, electronic, or mechanical, including photocopying, recording, or information storage and retrieval systems—without written permission from the publisher.

First Edition, 1978.
Second Edition, August 1994.

ISBN 0-87083-797-4

Published by

Living Stream Ministry
2431 W. La Palma Ave., Anaheim, CA 92801 U.S.A.
P. O. Box 2121, Anaheim, CA 92814 U.S.A.

Printed in the United States of America

98 99 00 01 02 03 04 / 10 9 8 7 6 5 4 3 2

CONTENTS

Title		Page
	Preface	v
1	A Mystery—Christ Magnified	1
2	The Way to Experience Christ	11
3	With One Soul	21
4	One in Soul	33
5	To Think the One Thing	41
6	Enjoying Christ by Repudiating the Flesh	51
7	The Excellency of the Knowledge of Christ and the Detailed Way to Experience Christ	59
8	Enjoying Christ by Counting All Things Loss	69
9	Attaining the Out-resurrection by Being Filled with Christ	77
10	In Him—the Secret of Experiencing Christ	85
11	Counting Gains Loss for Christ	93
12	The Excellency of the Knowledge of Christ	103
13	To Gain Christ and Be Found in Him	111
14	To Know Him	119
15	To Know the Power of His Resurrection	129
16	To Know the Fellowship of His Sufferings	137
17	Being Conformed to His Death	147
18	The All-accomplishing Death	157
19	Attaining unto the Out-resurrection	169
20	One Thing to Do	179
21	Dying to Live	189

| 22 | Cooperating with the Spirit | 199 |
| 23 | In the Empowering One | 207 |

PREFACE

This book is composed of messages given by Brother Witness Lee in the spring of 1978.

Chapter One

A MYSTERY—CHRIST MAGNIFIED

THE MYSTERY OF GOD

In the New Testament Christ has a particular title. Christians are familiar with many of the titles of Christ: Lord, Redeemer, Savior, Messiah, Son of God, Son of Man, the seed of woman, the seed of Abraham, the seed of David. But in Colossians 2:2 we see a very particular title of Christ—the mystery of God. According to the Greek, the last part of this verse reads, "To the acknowledgment of the mystery of God, even Christ." Christ is the mystery of God.

God is altogether a mystery. Nothing in the universe is as mysterious as God. Although God exists, no one has ever seen Him (John 1:18). However, God appeared to Abraham. How could God have appeared to Abraham without Abraham seeing Him? This certainly is not logical. Acts 7:2 says that the God of glory appeared to Abraham. Nevertheless, the Bible says that no one has ever seen God. This is a mystery.

In the Old Testament God appeared at least once in the form of a man. In Genesis 18 Abraham was sitting one day by the door of his tent, and he saw three men coming to him. Genesis 18:2 says, "And he lifted up his eyes and looked, and, lo, three men stood by him." One of these three was Jehovah. After greeting them, Abraham had a large meal prepared for them, a meal consisting of cakes, a calf, butter, and milk. Thus, Abraham not only saw God, but served Him a meal. How can we say that Abraham did not see God? Furthermore, according to Genesis 18, Abraham took a walk with Him and talked to Him. Therefore, when the Bible says that no one has ever seen God, it is a mystery.

Colossians 1:15 says that Christ is the image of the invisible God. Anything with an image must be visible. How then can the invisible God have a visible image? Is God visible or invisible? And how could He appear in the form of a man before the incarnation of Christ? Two thousand years before the incarnation, God appeared to Abraham in the form of a man. This is a mystery, and I cannot explain it. According to Colossians 2:2, Christ is the mystery of God. I cannot provide an adequate definition of this mystery. If I could, it would no longer be a mystery.

God is a mystery, and the mystery of God is Christ. In other words, God as a mystery is embodied in the Person of Christ. Therefore, Christ is the embodiment of God as the universal mystery. In all of history there is not another person as mysterious as Christ. He surely is mysterious. Today all nations use Christ's calendar. The calendar of all mankind is the calendar of the mystery of God.

THE MYSTERY OF CHRIST

Like Christ, the church also has a number of titles. The church is the gathering of the called ones, the household of God, the Body of Christ, and the one new man. According to Ephesians 3:4, the church also has a particular title—the mystery of Christ. When we consider Ephesians 3:4 in context, we see that the mystery of Christ is the church. Thus, Christ is the mystery of God, and the church is the mystery of Christ. God is a mystery, Christ is the mystery of God, and the church is the mystery of Christ. Hence, the church is actually a mystery within a mystery. The church is a mystery in the third stage. The first stage is God Himself as the mystery, the second is Christ as the mystery of God, and the third is the church as the mystery of Christ.

THE SPIRIT OF JESUS CHRIST

My burden in this message is not to share about the mystery; it is to have fellowship with you concerning the experience of the Christ who is the mystery of God. Christ is the center of all mysteries. Nevertheless, such a Christ can be experienced by us. In Philippians 1:19-26, for example, we see some mysteries. The first of these mysteries is found in verse 19: "For I know that this shall turn to my salvation through your prayer, and the bountiful supply of the Spirit of Jesus Christ" (Gk.). This Spirit is a mystery. Why does Paul here speak of the Spirit of Jesus Christ? Why does he not call this Spirit the Spirit of God or the Holy Spirit? No doubt, the Spirit here refers to the Holy Spirit. This is the only time in the entire Bible that the Spirit is called the Spirit of Jesus Christ. In Acts 16:7 we have the Spirit of Jesus (Gk.), and in Romans 8:9, the Spirit of Christ. But in this verse we do not have merely the Spirit of Jesus nor the Spirit of Christ, but the Spirit of Jesus Christ. This is a mystery, for we cannot adequately understand it.

CHRIST MAGNIFIED

A second mystery is found in verse 20: "According to my earnest expectation and my hope, that in nothing I shall be ashamed, but that with all boldness, as always, so now also Christ shall be magnified in my body, whether it be by life, or by death." We see here that no matter what was to happen to him, Paul's desire was that Christ would be magnified in his body. What does it mean for Christ to be magnified? Does it mean that Christ is made greater? Christ is already great. Does He then need to be enlarged? In Ephesians we are told that Christ fills all in all (1:23). How great He is! Many years ago some astronomers said that two hundred forty million solar systems form a galaxy and that forty billion galaxies form the unique center of the universe. Nevertheless, the Bible says that Christ fills all in all. Although Christ is so great, He still needs to be magnified.

In verse 21 Paul said, "For to me to live is Christ, and to die is gain." In verse 23 Paul said that his desire was to depart to be with Christ. In one verse Paul said that for him to live is Christ, but in another verse he said that he wanted to depart and be with Christ. At that time was Christ present with Paul, or was He absent from Paul? Christ surely was present with Paul. Why then did Paul still expect to be with Him? This is a mystery. The experience of Christ is altogether a mystery.

OUR CHRISTIAN LIVING BEING A MYSTERY

The more mysterious we are, the better. However, this

mystery must be our living, not a performance. Our Christian living is a mystery. Our Christian love and humility are also mysterious. The humility taught by Confucius was not a mystery. But when we Christians live out humility, this humility is mysterious. Whatever we live out from within us should be mysterious. Regarding our humility, others should say, "We cannot explain the kind of life this person lives. Although he is humble, his humility is different from that of others. His love is also different. It seems that he doesn't love anyone, but actually he loves others. His love is mysterious. There seems to be no limit to his love." Although human love is limited, the proper love lived out by a Christian is unlimited. Hence, it is a mystery.

Often I have heard people say, "I simply cannot tolerate this any more. This situation has exhausted my patience." If our patience can be exhausted, that indicates that it is not the patience of Christ. We Christians need to live out a patience that is unlimited. The more the circumstances exhaust our patience, the more patient we are, for our patience is inexhaustible. This is a mystery. It causes others to wonder how we can be so patient.

EXPRESSING CHRIST WITHOUT LIMITATION

To magnify Christ is to express Christ without limitation. It is to show to the whole universe that the very Christ who is our life and by whom we live is unlimited. According to the human concept, Christ is limited. But when people see us living by Him, they will realize that He is not limited. If the Apostle Paul had not been put in prison, no one would have understood how unlimited Christ was. It was through Paul's imprisonment that the Christ by whom Paul lived was expressed as the unlimited One. Because Paul's endurance was Christ Himself, it would have been impossible to exhaust his endurance no matter how long Paul had been kept in prison. Hence, it was inexhaustible and unlimited. Sometimes Christians ask others to pray for them because they are coming to the end of their endurance. Such endurance is not Christian endurance, for it is not endurance magnified. The Christ whom we experience as endurance cannot be exhausted. If we live by Him, He will be magnified; that is, He will show forth His inexhaustlessness. Because Paul's endurance was Christ, it was unlimited. Such an unlimited endurance is the magnification of the unlimited Christ. To the universe, this is a mystery.

Like endurance, our faithfulness, patience, and humility must also be unlimited. Any attribute we have through living by Christ will be unlimited and thus mysterious. By this we can see the difference between the human virtues and the virtues that are the magnification of Christ. All human virtues are limited. For example, human tolerance will eventually be exhausted. But the very magnification of Christ lived out of us cannot be exhausted. This mystery subdues the Devil, the demons, and all the evil angels. It also convinces everyone. Any proper human being will be convinced by seeing the magnification of Christ. Our Christian patience is a mystery because it is the magnification of Christ. This is not merely Christ manifested; it is Christ manifested as the unlimited One.

Even our forgiveness of others needs to be a magnification of Christ. In Matthew 18 Peter asked the Lord how many times he should forgive his brother. He asked if he should forgive him even seven times. But the Lord told him that he must forgive seventy times seven. This is inexhaustible forgiveness. Such forgiveness is the magnification of Christ. Our forgiveness is the inexhaustible Christ Himself. Again and again, throughout the years, we forgive others. This unlimited forgiveness is Christ magnified in us.

SUFFERING TO MAGNIFY CHRIST

Because the Christian virtues should be inexhaustible, often God will not reduce our sufferings. Rather, in order to magnify Christ, often He will increase them. In order to magnify Christ, it is necessary that we suffer. Suppose you pray, "O God, my Father, You are kind and merciful. You know that I cannot endure very much. Please reduce my suffering." If God answered your prayer and reduced your suffering, Christ would not be magnified. We need the sufferings for the manifestation of Christ. As our sufferings increase, Christ is magnified all the more. However, do not be concerned about what kind of suffering enables us to magnify Christ. Instead of analyzing this matter, we should simply love the Lord and experience Him.

When sufferings increase, we may think that our heavenly Father is cruel and merciless. Remember, this word about magnifying Christ was spoken by someone in prison. The longer he was in prison, the more he magnified Christ. To be magnified means to be enlarged. As we have pointed out, to magnify Christ means to express Him as the One who is unlimited. He is magnified through the increase of our sufferings. Do not be afraid of suffering, for it is a joy to magnify Christ through suffering. Many Christian teachers realize that the book of Philippians is a book of joy. Over and over again, in this book Paul tells us to rejoice in the Lord. When we are in a pleasant environment, it may not mean very much to be joyful. But to rejoice when we are in prison means a great deal.

THE SUM TOTAL OF OUR CHRISTIAN LIVING

The experience of Christ is a mystery, and whatever we experience of Christ is unlimited. If we see this vision, it will not only control our life, but also strengthen our Christian walk. God's intention is to magnify Christ through us. The church life is the sum total of our Christian living. We all live by Christ, and our Christian living is added together to make the church life. Our Christian life is a mystery, and whatever of Christ we live out is also a mystery. We all are mysterious because Christ lives in us. For example, we may speak by Christ, but our speaking by Christ is a mystery. Although it is a mystery, it is nonetheless a fact. What we are experiencing of Christ today is a mystery. Day by day, our living is mysterious. Thus, when we come together as the church, we are a complete mystery. The sum total of all these mysteries is the church life. This mystery manifests the One who is unlimited.

THE MYSTERY OF EXPERIENCING CHRIST

In order for Christ to be lived out by us, He must be in

us. Paul said, "For to me to live is Christ." This means that we can live to be Christ. As we are living to be Christ, we still expect to be with Him. Thus, Christ is present, yet absent. This also is a mystery showing that Christ is unlimited. Because we are limited, we cannot be both absent and present. The Christ we are experiencing is unlimited. Therefore, He can be present and absent.

The Christ whom we experience and by whom we live is different from what we think He is. Experiencing Christ and living by Him is a mystery. If you think that you are experiencing Christ, you may not be experiencing Him. But if you think that you are not experiencing Him, you are probably experiencing Him. As you are experiencing Christ, you may not sense that you are experiencing Him. He is not only mysterious, but also abstract, invisible, and intangible. When you feel like rejecting Christ and giving Him up, you have a certain sense within. This sense is different from the sense you have most of the time. Perhaps now you do not feel that you are experiencing Christ. You may feel that you are just experiencing yourself. Do not be robbed—you may actually be experiencing Christ. However, when you abandon Christ and give Him up, you have quite a different sense within. When you have that sense, then you can realize that you had been experiencing Christ. This shows that the experience of Christ is mysterious.

Those in the Pentecostal movement often try to make Christ someone who is not mysterious. But anything that is not mysterious is not real. If your experience is not mysterious, it is not the real experience of Christ. Christ is here, yet He is not here. It is the same with God. The Bible says that no man has ever seen Him, yet He has appeared to men. It is difficult to say whether Christ is abstract or concrete. People always try to make the mysterious Christ so concrete that He is no longer mysterious. This is a false performance.

In the past many of us have claimed to have had wonderful experiences. But after a certain period of time, we no longer thought that those experiences were wonderful. Rather, we realized that they were a performance. Although we may not have such so-called wonderful experiences in the church life, we cannot deny the fact that we have experienced Christ. We have experienced something that cannot be erased from our being. This is Christ as our mystery.

This type of mysterious experience produces the genuine growth in life. The so-called wonderful experiences actually do not help us to grow in life. It is these mysterious experiences of Christ that help us to grow.

The experience of Christ is altogether a mystery, and this experience is unlimited, for it is Christ magnified. Any experience that is not mysterious but is easily understood should be doubted. The genuine experiences cannot be understood; they are mysterious. Suppose someone would say, "I simply do not understand what happened to me yesterday. I can't tell whether or not I loved the Lord. I simply don't know. If I say that I loved the Lord, I will sense an accusation within that I did not love Him. But if I say that I didn't love the Lord, I would be telling a lie. I love the Lord, yet I dare not say that I love Him." This is a real experience. However, suppose someone says, "Praise the Lord! Yesterday, by the Lord's grace, I was very humble." This kind of humility is a performance. But, on the other hand, suppose someone says, "I couldn't tell whether I was humble or not. Maybe I was humble, but it also seemed to me that I was proud." This is a real experience of Christ as humility. This kind of experience of Christ is visible yet invisible, tangible yet intangible. Such an experience is unlimited; it is enduring because it is the magnification of Christ.

If you are certain that what you are experiencing is an experience of Christ, that is not normal, and you should question it. The only thing we can be sure of is our salvation. The more you are assured of salvation, the better. You should be able to say, "Praise the Lord that I have been saved! Heaven may pass away and the earth may be removed, but my salvation cannot be questioned. I have the full assurance of salvation." But the subtle enemy will not easily allow any to have the assurance of salvation. At every opportunity, he raises a question about this and causes doubt. But this doubt is the strongest assurance of salvation. If you have never doubted your salvation, it is an indication that you are probably not saved. Your doubt is the strongest confirmation and assurance that you are saved. Although Satan does not want us to have the assurance of salvation, he may push us to have the false assurance of other things. For example, some may say, "I have the assurance that I am an overcomer. Yesterday I received the assurance that I am among the firstfruit. By the Lord's grace, I am now one of the hundred forty-four thousand" (Rev. 14:1). We need to doubt this type of assurance. Do not have any assurance of your experience, for all experiences of Christ are mysterious. I believe that we all are now experiencing Christ, but in a mysterious way. The church is mysterious because the universal mystery is here. Thus, the church is a mystery within a mystery.

We magnify Christ by the bountiful supply of the Spirit of Jesus Christ. Although this supply is bountiful, it is not visible. We may not sense that the supply is bountiful; nevertheless, it is bountiful. Christ can never be exhausted. Many of us may feel that we are weak. But this weakness is a mysterious weakness, for actually we are not weak. Some, however, may claim to be strong. But their strength is not real. All the experiences of Christ are a mystery. This is the magnification of Christ.

When you sense that you are experiencing Christ, that may not be real. But when you doubt whether or not you are experiencing Christ, that may be real. The experience of Christ in our Christian life is mysterious. A mystery is something that we cannot understand or explain but that we can simply accept.

In Philippians 2 Paul said that he was ready to be poured out as a drink offering. That was to take place at the end of his race when he was martyred. In Philippians 3 Paul said that he had not yet attained, that he was forgetting the things that were behind and stretching forth to the things ahead to gain the prize of the high calling of God in Christ Jesus. Thus, at the time of writing the book of Philippians, Paul was still running the race. He did not have the assurance that he had obtained the prize. He had this assurance only at the time he was martyred. In 1 Corinthians 9 Paul said that he was running the race and fighting to subdue his body, lest after preaching to others he himself would be a castaway. First Corinthians was written rather early in his ministry, but Philippians was written close to the time of his martyrdom. If you read the writings of the Apostle Paul, you will see that, on the one hand, he had assurance and that, on the other hand, he did not have assurance. First Corinthians 7 reveals that the experience of Christ is mysterious. In this chapter the Apostle Paul said something by himself (v. 25). But at the end of the chapter he said, "And I think also that I have the Spirit of God."

The experience of Christ is both tangible and intangible, both abstract and concrete. God, Christ, the church life, and our Christian experience are all a mystery. We cannot make this mystery altogether solid, tangible, or visible. It would be foolish for us to try. The more mysterious we are, the better. If we do not have any experience, we shall not have any mysterious questionings about what is happening within us. The more we love Christ, pursue Him, and live by Him, the more we shall doubt whether or not we are actually experiencing Christ. This shows that our Christian life cannot be explained, for it is a mystery. The more mysterious we are, the more experiences of Christ we shall have. The entire matter of experiencing Christ is a mystery.

Chapter Two

THE WAY TO EXPERIENCE CHRIST

Most Christian teachers know that the book of Philippians is a book of experience. Philippians is a book on the experience of Christ. In the arrangement of the books of the New Testament, Philippians comes between Ephesians, a book on the Body, and Colossians, a book on the Head. Thus, between the Body and the Head we have the experience of Christ. This means that the way to get from the Body to the Head is through the experience of Christ. This is a strong indication that if we would know the Head, we must have the experience of Christ.

In Philippians Paul speaks about the experience of Christ in a very peculiar way. According to our concept, to experience Christ we must clear the past, consecrate ourselves to Christ, open to the inner anointing, and obey the anointing. Along with this, we need to pray a great deal and have fellowship with the Lord and with one another. This concept of experiencing Christ is not wrong. It is normal and very common. However, in Philippians Paul does not speak of the experience of Christ in this way. It took me more than forty years to understand the way Paul speaks of experiencing Christ in Philippians.

THE FELLOWSHIP IN THE GOSPEL

Philippians 1:5 says, "For your fellowship in the gospel from the first day until now," and verse 6 continues, "Being confident of this very thing, that he which hath begun a good work in you will perform it until the day of Jesus Christ." These verses indicate that the fellowship in the gospel is a good work, a work initiated by Christ. Christ will perform this work until the day of Jesus Christ. Philippians unveils the fact that the experience of Christ is the fellowship in the gospel until the Lord Jesus comes back. Notice that in verse 5 Paul does not speak of the preaching of the gospel, but of the fellowship in the gospel. Have you ever noticed that there is such a term in the New Testament as the fellowship in the gospel? No doubt you have heard of the fellowship of the Spirit, for this is very common. The fellowship of the Spirit is in our concept, but the fellowship in the gospel is not. From the time we are saved until the time the Lord Jesus comes back, our Christian life should be a gospel-preaching life. We are not here for our education, job, or family, and we are not here to earn money or to gain a reputation or position. We are here to live a gospel-preaching life, a life that preaches Christ. Our living should be our preaching. If someone asks your profession, you should say, "My profession is preaching the gospel." Thus, our life is primarily a gospel-preaching life. Whether I speak or remain silent, my life, my living, my being, and my entire person are a preaching of Christ.

Our gospel-preaching life should not be individualistic; rather, it must be corporate. This is the reason that in the preaching of the gospel we have fellowship. The word fellowship is rich in meaning. The Greek word rendered fellowship, *koinonia,* means communication, mutual interchange. As far as the preaching of the gospel is concerned, today's situation is very poor. Either Christians do not preach the gospel or they preach it individualistically, not corporately. Every evangelist is individualistic. It seems that the more evangelistic people are, the more individualistic they are. In their preaching of the gospel there is no fellowship. Because there is no fellowship in the gospel, there is no experience of Christ.

Even if we clear the past, consecrate ourselves to the Lord, and follow the inner anointing, we still may not necessarily have that much experience of Christ. But if we preach the gospel in a corporate way, we shall be full of the experience of Christ. The book of Philippians does not speak of clearing the past, consecration, or the anointing. But it does speak of the fellowship in the gospel. I am very glad that many among us are zealous for the preaching of the gospel on the campuses. But I wonder if in this preaching of the gospel there is the fellowship in the gospel. If we simply engage in the preaching of the gospel, we shall not have very much experience of Christ. The experience of Christ is not mainly in the preaching; it is in the fellowship. We need to preach the gospel in fellowship. As long as you have fellowship in your preaching of the gospel, you will experience Christ.

ENVY, STRIFE, AND RIVALRY

We human beings are not simple, but complicated and intricate. In chapter one of Philippians, a chapter on the fellowship in the gospel, Paul says that some preach Christ out of envy, strife, and rivalry (vv. 15-16). Some may say, "Last month I brought more people to the Lord than you did. Among those I brought to the Lord were a professor and an outstanding student." Even those in the same church may strive against one another in preaching the gospel. Furthermore, we may also compete with churches in other cities. Thus, after strife comes rivalry. Even in something as divine as the preaching of Christ, it is possible to have rivalry.

Those on the same campus engaged in preaching the gospel may have rivalry among them concerning who will be the leader. Those who cannot be first will at least desire to be second. How disappointed they would be to be last! Such rivalry is hidden within us. When we have such rivalry, we do not have fellowship in the gospel. In your schoolwork it is all right to be zealous to be first, but not in the preaching of the gospel. Rather, in the preaching of the gospel, you should be willing to be nothing. Those who preach Christ out of envy, strife, and rivalry certainly do not have fellowship in the gospel. If we do not have fellowship, we cannot have the experience of Christ.

I am very happy that the young people are zealous to preach the gospel on the campuses. But now I must ask whether or not in their preaching of the gospel they have the experience of Christ. This depends upon whether or not they have the fellowship in the gospel. It is not a simple matter to have this fellowship. It requires that we put ourselves, our ambition, our reputation, and our position aside. This is a real killing. The fellowship in the gospel kills the self, the flesh, and the natural man. It also kills our ambition, desire, preference, and choice. This is the reason that the fellowship in the preaching of the gospel causes us to experience Christ. Thus, according to the word of the Apostle Paul in Philippians, the first way to experience Christ is in the fellowship of the gospel.

THE BOUNTIFUL SUPPLY OF THE SPIRIT OF JESUS CHRIST

The second way is through the bountiful supply of the Spirit of Jesus Christ (Phil. 1:19). Notice that in Philippians 1:19 Paul speaks not of the Spirit of God, the Spirit of Jesus, or the Spirit of Christ, but of the Spirit of Jesus Christ. Not many Christians are familiar with the significance of this title. In Genesis 1:2 we have the term the Spirit of God. Other books in the Old Testament speak of the Spirit of Jehovah. The Spirit of Jehovah fell upon certain prophets. (The King James Version always renders this "the Spirit of the Lord.") In the New Testament we find the term the Holy Spirit. This term is not used in the Old Testament because it is related to the incarnation of Christ. At the time Christ was conceived in Mary, the angel said, "The Holy Spirit shall come upon thee, and the power of the Highest shall overshadow thee" (Luke 1:35). According to Matthew 1:20, the angel of the Lord told Joseph that what had been begotten in Mary was of the Holy Spirit. Therefore, firstly there is the Spirit of God, then the Spirit of Jehovah, and then the Holy Spirit. The Spirit of God is related to God's creation, the Spirit of Jehovah is related to God's relationship with man, and the Holy Spirit is related to the Son of God becoming a man. John 7:39 says, "The Spirit was not yet." What Spirit was not yet? This refers to the Spirit of the glorified Jesus that was "not yet" until the time of Jesus' resurrection. After Jesus' glorification, the Spirit of God, which is the Spirit of Jehovah and the Holy Spirit, became the Spirit of Jesus Christ.

According to the Greek, in Acts 16:7 we find the term the Spirit of Jesus, and in Romans 8:9, the term the Spirit of

Christ. If you read Acts 16, you will see that the Spirit of Jesus is related mainly to the preaching of the gospel. It was not the Spirit of God or the Spirit of Christ but the Spirit of Jesus that did not allow them to go into Mysia. The Spirit of Christ is found in Romans 8, a chapter on resurrection life. Therefore, the Spirit of Christ is related to resurrection. In Philippians 1:19 these two terms, the Spirit of Jesus and the Spirit of Christ, are combined in the term the Spirit of Jesus Christ. The Spirit of Jesus Christ is for the experience of Christ.

ONE IN SOUL BY THE SPIRIT OF JESUS

The first two chapters of Philippians are related to the Spirit of Jesus, and the last two are related to the Spirit of Christ. Chapters one and two are related not to resurrection, but to Jesus. But chapters three and four are related to resurrection. For example, Philippians 3:10 says, "To know him and the power of his resurrection" (Gk.). Furthermore, Philippians 4:13 says, "I can do all things in him who empowers me" (Gk.). This is the Spirit of Christ, who is related to resurrection. In the first chapter of Philippians we have the preaching of the gospel. To preach the gospel we need the Spirit of Jesus. The Spirit of Jesus is clearly portrayed in the first two chapters. The Spirit of Jesus does not strive, and it has no rivalry or enmity. When Jesus, the Nazarene, was on earth, He did not have any envy, strife, or rivalry. These three negative things are mentioned in chapter one. In this chapter there are also some positive things, such as the fellowship and the matter of being in one spirit and one soul. How can we have one spirit and one soul? This is not possible by our spirit, for our spirit is a spirit of envy. When we see others taking the lead, we are envious. Then we begin to strive in the spirit of rivalry. Although our spirit is like this, the Spirit of Jesus is not. Consider the life of Jesus as presented in the Gospels. His life was a life without envy, strife, or rivalry. To be one in spirit and in soul is possible only in the Spirit of Jesus.

To be one soul mainly means to be one mind. The reason Christians cannot be one soul is that each desires to be first and that no one is willing to be last. But it is possible for us to be one soul by the Spirit of Jesus. If we say, "I want to be in the Spirit of Jesus," we shall immediately have the experience of Christ and be one spirit and one soul with others. Then we shall strive together for the gospel. The word "together" in Philippians 1:27 means that we are coordinated and that we are not individualistic, but corporate. When we are all in the Spirit of Jesus and are in one soul, we shall strive together.

Although the first chapter of Philippians is rather long, it may be outlined quite simply. This chapter is concerned with the fellowship in the gospel by the Spirit of Jesus without envy, strife, or rivalry. It is in this way that we experience Christ. It is not simply a matter of clearing the past, consecrating ourselves, or caring for the inner anointing. That is not the way from the Body to the Head. In order to reach the Head, we need the fellowship in the gospel by the Spirit of Jesus without envy, strife, or rivalry. In our gospel-preaching life there should be no envy, strife, or rivalry, not even with the opposers. Instead, we should simply preach the gospel by the Spirit of Jesus. But as long as there is the slightest bit of rivalry, we cannot be in the Spirit of Jesus. Moreover, if we are not in the Spirit of Jesus, we are not in the fellowship of the gospel, and we are through with the experience of Christ. To experience Christ we need the fellowship in the gospel by the Spirit of Jesus without envy, strife, or rivalry.

HAVING THE SAME LOVE

Now we come to Philippians chapter two. The first verse says, "If there be therefore any encouragement in Christ, if any comfort of love, if any fellowship of spirit, if any tender mercies and compassions" (Gk.). It took me more than thirty years to understand this verse. Verse 2 indicates that in saying all this, the Apostle Paul was begging the saints in Philippi to make his joy full. Paul seemed to be saying, "Please make my joy full. Do you have a tender heart? Do you have compassion toward me? Your strife and rivalry have made me sorrowful. If you do have tender mercies, if you have encouragement and trust, if you have some comfort of love toward me, if you have any fellowship of spirit with me, please make my joy full."

Verse 2 says, "Fulfill ye my joy, that ye think the same thing, having the same love, one in soul, thinking the one thing" (Gk.). In this verse Paul was beseeching the Philippians to think the same thing and to have the same love. We should not have special friendships, but have the same love toward one another. In his latter years, the Apostle Paul, who was soon to be poured out to the Lord as a drink offering, was asking the Philippians to make his joy full by having the same love toward everyone. If Paul had heard that the Philippians had the same love, he would have been very happy. But because they had a different love for various people, he was sorrowful, for that kind of love caused them to lose the oneness and to be out of the fellowship of the gospel.

ONE IN SOUL

Verse 2 also speaks of being one in soul. To be one in soul means to be one in our affection, love, thought, and decisions. Such oneness is very practical. If we want to experience Christ, we need to be one in soul. If we are not one in our affections, thoughts, and decisions, we are not one in soul. As long as we are not one in soul, we are not in the fellowship of the gospel.

THE SPIRIT OF JESUS
AND THE FELLOWSHIP IN THE GOSPEL

Verse 3 says, "Let nothing be done through rivalry or vainglory; but in lowliness of mind let each esteem other better than themselves" (Gk.). To desire a high position among the saints is vainglory. We should not do anything in the way of rivalry or vainglory, in the way of seeking glory for ourselves. Rather, in lowliness of mind, we should esteem others as surpassing us. This is the way to experience Christ and to stay in the fellowship in the gospel. Although we may preach the gospel, we may not have the fellowship in the gospel because we esteem ourselves higher than others.

In verse 4 Paul says, "Look not every man on his own

things, but every man also on the things of others." The word "things" in this verse means virtues, attributes, or qualities. We are accustomed to looking on our own virtues, but not on the virtues of others. Thus, Paul said that we should look not just on our own qualities, but also on the qualities of others.

Verses 5 and 6 continue, "Let this mind be in you, which was also in Christ Jesus: who, being in the form of God, thought it not robbery to be equal with God." Christ was equal to God; He did not rob God of His position. However, often we commit robbery. For example, we may want to be first, but not have the necessary qualifications. In this way we rob others of what is theirs. A brother may not be qualified to be an elder, yet he desires to be an elder. Thus, he robs those who are qualified for the eldership because he desires something he is not equal to. But if someone is equal to the eldership and wants to have it, that is not robbery. Christ was God. Therefore, for Him to be equal with God was not robbery. But for us to desire to be an apostle like Paul is robbery. In doing this, we rob Paul of his apostleship.

In verses 7 through 9 we are told that Christ emptied Himself, took upon Himself the form of a slave, and was made in the likeness of men. Found in fashion as a man, He humbled Himself and became obedient unto death, even to the death of the cross. This is the Spirit of Jesus. In verse 9 Paul says that God has exalted Christ and has given Him a name above every other name. Thus, according to verse 10, "At the name of Jesus every knee should bow." All this is related to the Spirit of Jesus. For the preaching of the gospel we need this Spirit.

Our life should be a life of gospel preaching. In our preaching of the gospel, we need the Spirit of Jesus. In this Spirit there is no envy, strife, rivalry, robbery, or looking at our own qualities. Rather, in the Spirit of Jesus, we look on the qualities of others. This is the Spirit of Jesus for the experience of Christ. If we have this Spirit, we shall be in the fellowship of the gospel, and our preaching of the gospel will be prevailing and fruitful. Furthermore, our fellowship will be full of the enjoyment of Christ. This is the way to enjoy

Christ and to experience Him all day long. This is possible by the bountiful supply of the Spirit of Jesus Christ. When we have no envy, strife, or rivalry, but stay in the bountiful supply of the Spirit of Jesus Christ, there is no need for us to try to experience Christ. We shall experience Him spontaneously.

Chapter Three

WITH ONE SOUL

We have seen that the book of Philippians is a book on the experience of Christ. This fact is recognized by most Christian teachers. Many Christians point to Paul's word in Philippians 3 about counting all things loss for Christ and knowing Christ, the power of His resurrection, and the fellowship of His sufferings. But I do not know of any who have pointed out the fellowship in the gospel and the Spirit of Jesus Christ. The way to experience Christ is not firstly to know the power of His resurrection. It is firstly to participate in the fellowship in the gospel by the Spirit of Jesus Christ.

PROBLEMS WITH THE SOUL

Both the fellowship in the gospel and the Spirit of Jesus Christ are unusual expressions. Chapter one contains other unusual expressions, such as "in one spirit, with one soul striving together for the faith of the gospel" (v. 27, Gk.). It is rather easy for us to understand the expression "in one spirit," but not the phrase "with one soul." The translators of the King James Version rendered this "with one mind." They interpreted the Greek word used here, *psuche,* as mind. The first problem we have with our soul is with our mind. This is especially true of the brothers. The second main part of the soul is the emotion. This presents a special problem to the sisters. Regarding our soul, we are also troubled by our stubborn will. Thus, in our soul we have a troublesome mind, a perplexing emotion, and a stubborn will.

The soul is the most intricate and complicated part of our being. As tripartite creatures, we have a body, a soul, and a spirit. Although our body has many members and is difficult to take care of, it is not as perplexing to us as our soul is. The simplest part of our being is our spirit. The part of us that troubles us the most is our soul. Tears, for example, do not issue from our spirit. The sisters' tears come from their emotion, and the brothers' tears come from their mind. I can assure the brothers that if we did not think so much, we would not have any tears. For the brothers, the mind is the fountain of tears. The most thoughtful people suffer the most. Those who think a great deal commit suicide more often than those who are simple. When certain thoughtful people find no way to go on in life, they commit suicide.

Our mind and emotion need tuning. But our stubborn will frustrates this tuning. There is nothing wrong with having a thoughtful mind and a sensitive emotion, but they need to be adjusted by our will. However, our will is stubborn. We need to use our will as a brake to restrict our emotion. But often this brake does not seem to work because our will is stubborn. Whenever we lose control of our emotion, it means that our will is not functioning properly. Some sisters seem to have only an emotion, not a will. Likewise, certain brothers seem to have only a mind and not a will. We need to use our will to control our mind and our emotion.

In writing Philippians 1:27, Paul did not say "with one mind"; he said "with one soul." The mind does not include all the problems we have with our soul. The mind, emotion, and will all give us difficulties. Therefore, in translating Philippians 1:27, it is better to say "with one soul." In order to be one soul, we must not remain in our mind, emotion, and will.

The problem with the experience of Christ is not mainly with our spirit, but with our soul. Those outside the Lord's recovery, however, may have a problem with their spirit because few know anything about the spirit or how to exercise their spirit. Many have only an objective Christ, a Christ far away in the heavens, and do not know the Christ who is in their spirit. They have no idea that Christ as the life-giving Spirit is now indwelling their spirit. But we who have been in the church life for a number of years are somewhat familiar with the spirit. With us, the problem in experiencing Christ is mainly with our soul. In the past we have laid great emphasis upon the spirit. But simply to speak of the spirit in the experience of Christ is not adequate, for we have not only a spirit, but also a soul.

THE EXPERIENCE OF CHRIST AND THE ENJOYMENT OF CHRIST

At this point we can make a distinction between the experience of Christ and the enjoyment of Christ. The experience of Christ is a matter primarily in our spirit, but the enjoyment of Christ is in our soul. To experience Christ is one thing, and to enjoy Christ is another. Consider the example of eating food. It is one thing to eat food and another thing to enjoy it. Sometimes parents force their children to eat certain foods. Although the children may eat out of the fear of being disciplined, they do not enjoy the food they are eating. Rather, they suffer as they eat. Sometimes we experience Christ, not in the way of enjoyment, but in the way of suffering. We may say, "I must take Christ as my life and live by Him. I have to experience Christ." But this is not the enjoyment of Christ. Like children who eat without enjoying their food, many times we experience Christ without enjoying Him. Instead of enjoying Christ, we suffer. Thus, we can have the experience of Christ without the enjoyment of Christ. The problem here is with our soul.

THE BACKGROUND OF THE BOOK OF PHILIPPIANS

Before we consider this matter further, let us consider the background of the book of Philippians. No doubt, the saints in Philippi were very good. They were zealous for the gospel, and they were very much for the Lord. In chapter four we see that they cared for the needs of the Apostle Paul a number of times. To take care of the needs of the Lord's servant is very significant. If you are not truly for the Lord, you will not take care of the needs of His servant. Taking care of the needs of the Lord's servant is a strong proof and sign that you are for the Lord. Although the Philippians were zealous for the gospel, were for the Lord, and took care of the Apostle's need, they still had a problem regarding oneness. Instead of being one, they were quite opinionated. The sisters especially had a problem with opinions. This is the reason Paul says, "I beseech Euodias, and beseech Syntyche, that they think the same thing in the Lord" (4:2, Gk.). Euodias and Syntyche, two of the leading sisters, were not one. In most churches the discord occurs mainly among the sisters. If there had not been so many opinions among the Philippians, the Apostle Paul would not have repeatedly told them to think the same thing (2:2; 4:2). According to the Greek, Philippians 2:5 should be rendered, "Think this among you which was also in Christ Jesus." This means that in our thinking we need to be one with Christ. It is not simply a matter of the mind, but of the working of the mind, the process of thinking. The saints in Philippi were good, honest, and faithful, but they were too opinionated. Because of this, they did not have the adequate enjoyment of Christ. When we read this book carefully, we see that this was the situation among them.

Strictly speaking, Philippians is a book not only on the experience of Christ, but also on the enjoyment of Christ. In Philippians 3:8 Paul said that for the sake of Christ he counted all things dung. This is not only a matter of experience, but also a matter of enjoyment. The excellency of the knowledge of Christ (3:8) also indicates enjoyment. Excellency is not mainly for experience, but for enjoyment. In chapter three Paul seemed to be saying, "Formerly, I, Saul of Tarsus, enjoyed my status. I was a Hebrew of the Hebrews and a Pharisee. But now I count all things loss for Christ." The dung, the dog food mentioned in verse 8, indicates no enjoyment. No human being can have enjoyment from dog food. Therefore, the book of Philippians is concerned not only with the experience of Christ, but also with the enjoyment of Christ. With the enjoyment of Christ there is a pleasant taste.

Although the Philippians were good, they had lost their enjoyment of Christ. They may have had a proper spirit, but there was a problem in their soul. They might have been one in spirit, but they were definitely not one in soul. This is the background of this Epistle.

Every Epistle in the New Testament was written for a particular reason. The reason for writing the Epistle to the Philippians was that, although they were for the Lord and cared for His servant and were very good in their spirit, they had a problem in their soul because they did not think the same thing. In their thinking they had a problem. Hence, Paul wrote this Epistle to advise them and even to beg them to be one in soul.

LOSING THE ENJOYMENT OF CHRIST

Our need today is very similar to that of the Philippians. In chapter one Paul said of the Philippians, "I thank my God upon every remembrance of you, always in every prayer of mine for you all making request with joy" (vv. 3-4). I feel the same way toward all the dear saints in the Lord's recovery. I can sincerely say that I praise the Lord for all the saints. Nevertheless, I am somewhat concerned that you may not have very much enjoyment of Christ. Perhaps when you first arrived in your locality, you had considerable enjoyment of Him. But as time has gone by you may have lost this enjoyment. The reason for this is that there is a problem in the soul. Either the sisters are too much in the emotion, or the brothers are too much in the mind. But we all have a problem with our stubborn will. My burden is that this stubborn will would be dealt with. Many of those who have been in the Lord's recovery a long time are like children eating food without enjoying it. When they first came, everything was enjoyable, but many do not have this enjoyment today. The reason many lose the enjoyment of Christ is the problem they have in the soul. The young people may be very active in preaching the gospel on the campuses. They may pray, praise, and shout hallelujah. But all this may become merely the carrying out of a duty. There may not be much enjoyment of Christ. If you do not have much enjoyment of Christ, it indicates that you are not one in soul. Your thoughts and emotions differ from those of others. The reason Euodias and Syntyche were not one was that they had a problem in the soul. They were not thinking the same thing.

THINKING ONE THING

It seems that it is impossible for us all to think one thing. Nevertheless, the Bible charges us to do this. Paul's word in

Philippians about thinking one thing is not history. In other words, he was not telling us how the Philippian believers were thinking one thing. On the contrary, it is a word of advice. In our humanity it is impossible for us to carry out Paul's advice. But it is possible by the Spirit of Jesus. If we live by the Spirit of Jesus and not by our soul, we shall be able to think one thing. Notice that Paul does not say to praise concerning one thing, or to pray one thing. To praise and pray are matters in the spirit. Thinking, however, is a matter in the soul. As we have seen, the hindrance to enjoying Christ is not in our spirit, but in our soul. And the problem is mainly not with our stubborn will or perplexing emotion, but with our troublesome mind. But our mind is affected by our emotion and will. If our emotion is not finely tuned and if our will is not subdued, we shall not think properly.

DEALING WITH THE SOUL
FOR THE ENJOYMENT OF CHRIST

For years, we have spoken about the experience of Christ and the enjoyment of Christ, but we have not seen the detailed way to enjoy Christ. Therefore, l have been burdened to give a number of messages on the way to enjoy Christ. In order to enjoy Him, we need to deal with every part of our soul, especially with our mind. If our way of thinking is dealt with, we shall have the proper taste for Christ and we shall both experience Him and enjoy Him. We shall not only eat, but enjoy what we are eating. Whether or not we enjoy the food we eat depends upon our taste. Concerning Christ, our taste is mainly with our soul. This is the reason that concerning the experience of Christ and the enjoyment of Christ, we need to deal with the various parts of our soul.

CONDUCT WORTHY OF THE GOSPEL

The last part of Philippians 1 and the first part of Philippians 2 are actually one portion and should not be separated. One thought flows from 1:27 through 2:8. In 1:27 Paul says, "Only let your conduct be worthy of the gospel of Christ" (Gk.). When I read this verse years ago, I thought that conduct worthy of the gospel was behavior that was perfect before those to whom we preach the gospel. But this is not Paul's meaning here. The remainder of verse 27 says, "That whether I come and see you, or else be absent, I may hear of your affairs, that ye stand fast in one spirit, with one soul striving together for the faith of the gospel." (Gk.). Paul does not speak here of loving our wives, submitting to our husbands, honoring our parents, or behaving in a kind, lovable manner. Rather, he tells us to stand fast in one spirit with one soul. If we are not in one spirit with one soul, then our conduct is not worthy of the gospel. No matter how many of us there may be in a locality or on a campus, in our preaching of the gospel everyone must be fully impressed that we are in one spirit and with one soul. Nothing is more convincing than this. When all the members in the church are in one spirit with one soul, this oneness will be convincing, subduing, and attractive. When we have such a subduing and convincing oneness, we shall experience Christ and enjoy Him. We shall enjoy Christ by being in one spirit with one soul. By preaching the gospel we express our oneness in spirit and in soul. When we preach the gospel in this way, we have the enjoyment of Christ. The more we preach like this, the more we enjoy Christ. We shall be able to say, "We don't care mainly for how many souls are saved, or for how many people are brought to the Lord. We are enjoying the Lord." We shall be full of enjoyment, and the preaching of the gospel will be a feast. But if we do not sense that we are feasting on Christ as we preach the gospel, something is wrong. We lack the oneness in spirit and in soul. But if we are in one spirit with one soul, the number of people saved through our preaching of the gospel will be secondary. The primary thing is that in the course of our preaching, we shall be feasting on Christ and enjoying Him. We shall have not only experience, but also enjoyment.

Verse 29 says, "For unto you it is given in the behalf of Christ, not only to believe on him, but also to suffer for his sake." Although in this verse Paul speaks of suffering, in reality to suffer for the sake of Christ is to enjoy Him. When we suffer for Christ's sake in the preaching of the gospel, we enjoy Him.

PAUL'S REQUEST

The concept expressed in the last part of chapter one continues in the first part of chapter two. Verse 1 says, "If there be therefore any encouragement in Christ, if any comfort of love, if any fellowship of spirit, if any tender mercies and compassions" (Gk.). When Paul spoke of encouragement here, he was speaking of encouragement to himself. He seemed to be saying, "I am suffering a great deal. You have heard of my suffering in prison. I hope that you have some encouragement for me in Christ. I also hope that you have some comfort of love, some fellowship of spirit, and some tender mercies and compassion." Verse 2 continues, "Fulfill ye my joy, that ye think the same thing, having the same love, one in soul, thinking the one thing" (Gk.). In this verse Paul asked the Philippians to make his joy full. This means that their situation should not be one that troubled him. Paul seemed to be saying, "Your situation bothers me. Although you preach the gospel, you are not one. I am suffering in prison for this gospel, but you are not one. Your lack of oneness does not encourage me; it troubles me. It does not comfort me or give me the proper fellowship. You are not showing mercy to me because you are bothering me. Don't you Philippians believe that you should have some mercy toward me and have some compassion on me? I beg you to fulfill my joy."

Paul was not asking the Philippians to fulfill his joy by sending him more offerings or by endeavoring to do something to secure his release from prison. That would not have been a comfort to him. What would have comforted Paul was that the Philippians would think the same thing, have the same love, be one in soul, and think the one thing. Paul seemed to say, "If you do these things, you will be merciful to me, and you will be an encouragement to me. Such oneness will be a genuine comfort of love to me. But now you are not one. Thus, you are killing me. I beg you to be merciful to me. I am like an old father, and you are like my dear children. Your fighting with one another troubles me very much." This was Paul's concept in verses 1 and 2.

HAVING THE SAME LOVE

In verse 2 we find not only the matter of the mind, but also the matter of the emotion, for love is a matter of emotion. In verse 2 Paul implores the Philippians to have the same love. Thus, they were not only to think the same thing in their mind, but to have the same love in their emotion. Many among us today do not have the same love. Instead, our love for certain ones is on a higher level than our love for others. This is especially true among the sisters. The love among the sisters is on different levels. They love certain ones more and others less. This means that the sisters do not have the same love. To love the Apostle Paul above the other saints is wrong. We should love all the believers with the same love.

Paul's word about having the same love is a weighty word. It is a strong indication that the Philippians had a love that was on different levels. Our situation today is the same. Yes, we love one another, but our love differs, and the temperature of our love is not the same. When we contact certain ones, we are like ice, but when we contact others, we are like boiling water. For some, our love is too cold; for others, it is too hot. Our love should be moderate toward everyone. It should be neither too hot nor too cold. Sometimes people have told me that they love me. But within I said, "Your love is so cold. The more you love me, the colder I become. But your love for others is boiling hot."

To have a love that fluctuates in its temperature is to have a love that issues out of our natural life. Such a love comes from a soul that has not been dealt with. We can never enjoy Christ in this kind of love. If our love toward the saints has been regulated and dealt with, then we shall enjoy Christ as we love the saints. Whether or not our love is proper depends on whether or not we enjoy Christ in our loving of others. If you love others without having the enjoyment of Christ in that love, your love is wrong. It is neither moderate nor proper.

Are you sure that your love for the saints is all on one level? If not, then your love has honey in it. Honey was prohibited from being added to the meal offering because it could be easily leavened (Lev. 2:11). To be leavened means to be corrupted. Likewise, our natural love is easily corrupted.

Because there are no wasted words in the Bible, there must have been a reason for the Apostle Paul to write such a word as is found in Philippians 2:2. As we have pointed out, Paul seemed to be saying, "Philippians, do you have any tender mercy toward me? If you do, make my joy full by thinking the same thing, by having the same love, and by being one in soul. Do you intend to sympathize with me in my sufferings for the gospel in prison? Then you should not be so opinionated, and you should not be fighting against one another. This troubles me and hurts me. I beg you to think the same thing, to have the same love, and be one in soul. If you do this, you will fulfill my joy."

NO RIVALRY OR VAINGLORY

Verse 3 says, "Let nothing be done by the way of rivalry or vainglory; but in lowliness of mind let each esteem other better than themselves" (Gk.). According to this verse, there must have been rivalry and the seeking of vainglory among the Philippians. This is not the way to enjoy Christ. The enjoyment of Christ has nothing to do with rivalry or vainglory. If we do anything by the way of rivalry or vainglory, we are through with the experience of Christ.

LOOKING ON THE QUALITIES OF OTHERS

Verse 4 says, "Look not every man on his own qualities, but every man also on those of others" (Gk.). No doubt, some of the Philippians were looking on their own qualities, on their own good points. But Paul was telling them to look also on the qualities of others. Then, according to the Greek, in verse 5 Paul said, "Think this, which was also in Christ Jesus." In other words, Paul was telling them to think whatever Christ thought. This is the way for us to enjoy Christ.

HAVING A CO-SOUL

In this message we have seen the detailed way to enjoy Christ. First, we need to preach the gospel in the fellowship of the gospel. In order to keep ourselves in the fellowship of the gospel, we need to deal with our soul and be one in soul. Actually, the Greek word translated "one in soul" in Philippians 2:2 should be translated "co-soul." We all need to have the same soul. The problem today is that we do not have a co-soul. Thus, we are one in spirit, but we are different in soul. We can pray, praise, and sing together because all this is in the spirit. But we may not be able to talk together. This indicates that we are one in spirit, but not one in soul. In the meetings we have a co-spirit, but in our daily walk we do not have a co-soul. For the enjoyment of Christ, we need such a co-soul. We need to be together in the soul as well as in the spirit.

Chapter Four

ONE IN SOUL

In the first message we saw that Philippians is a book on the experience of Christ. Chapter one reveals that the way to experience Christ is through keeping ourselves in the fellowship in the gospel by the bountiful supply of the Spirit of Jesus Christ. If we would remain in the fellowship in the gospel by the bountiful supply of the Spirit of Jesus Christ, we need to be in one spirit with one soul. In Philippians the special point regarding the experience of Christ is this matter of being with one soul. Being one in soul is not only for the experience of Christ, but even the more for the enjoyment of Christ. Our experience of Christ should also be an enjoyment of Christ. For example, children may eat food under the threat of being disciplined if they do not eat, but they may not enjoy what they are eating. Likewise, if we are merely in one spirit, we may experience Christ and yet not enjoy Him. To experience Christ with enjoyment we need to be in one spirit with one soul.

A PROPER SOUL

According to the Bible, the soul is for enjoyment. To have enjoyment, we need desires, emotions, and feelings. The more emotional we are, the more we shall long for enjoyment. Enjoyment is mainly related to the soul. In order to enjoy Christ, we need to have a proper soul, a soul that is one with the souls of other saints. We need to ask ourselves whether we are many souls or just one soul.

Every soul has an opinion. If in one place there are five hundred souls, then there will be five hundred opinions. However, if we all have different opinions, we shall lose our enjoyment. If everyone in a family, for example, has the same opinion, that family will have a wonderful time of enjoyment. But if the father, the mother, and the children have different opinions, there will be no enjoyment in that family. When we all have one opinion, the situation among us will be heavenly.

If we do not have any opinions, we are not human. To be human is to be opinionated. Opinion, however, is not a bad word. In the Bible, a human being is not called a spirit or a body, but a soul. For example, the Bible says that seventy souls of the family of Jacob went down to Egypt (Gen. 46:27). Furthermore, the New Testament says that three thousand souls were added (Acts 2:41). Thus, a person is a soul. The basic element of the soul is opinion. Therefore, if you had no opinions, you would not be a soul. The strongest person is the one who has the strongest opinions. By a person's opinions you can know how strong he is psychologically.

THE REASON FOR THE WRITING OF THIS EPISTLE

Of all the churches in the New Testament, the best church was the church at Philippi. This church was fully established; it was in sound order. In the beginning of his Epistle to the Philippians, Paul addressed the saints, the bishops, and the deacons. This indicates that the church at Philippi had been established. The elders were not merely elders, but also bishops. All the saints in the church were zealous for the gospel and for the Lord's interests. Furthermore, those in this church took care of the needs of the Apostle Paul. The church in Philippi was much different from the church in Corinth, which was a mess, with lawsuits, fornication, and debates about doctrine, the Lord's table, and the spiritual gifts. But in Philippi everything was very good. Why then was this book written? Paul wrote this book because the Philippians were not one in their way of thinking. Rather, there was discord among them. In other words, they were not one in soul. As we have seen, they did not have the same love for one another. Therefore, Paul encouraged them to have the same love. To some brothers and sisters their love was hot, but to others it was cold. We can sympathize with the Apostle Paul because among us today we have different levels of love, not the same love. The Philippians had problems both in the mind and in the emotion. Because of these problems, the Epistle to the Philippians was written.

PAUL'S REQUEST

As we have seen, in the second chapter of this book Paul begged the Philippians to sympathize with him. Paul seemed to be saying, "If you have any encouragement in Christ toward me, any comfort of love, any fellowship of spirit, any tender mercy and compassion, please make my joy full." Paul was very sorrowful over the discord among the Philippians. But in wisdom he did not tell them how sorrowful he was. Instead, he spoke a positive word, asking them to encourage him and to have mercy upon him. In asking this, he was implying that their discord was causing him to suffer. Paul seemed to be saying, "Do not cause me further hurt by your discord. Be merciful to me. If you have mercy on me, an old man in prison for the sake of the gospel, you will fulfill my joy by thinking the same thing and by having the same love. Oh, Philippian brothers, I am weeping in prison for you because you are not in one accord, because you are not one in mind and in soul. I beg you to have compassion toward me. I need your compassion to heal the wound within my heart which has been caused by the discord among you. Please make my joy full. When you think the same thing and have the same love, my joy will be made full."

The Greek prefix in the phrase "one soul" in verse 2 may also be translated "together." Paul was telling the Philippians that they needed to be together in their soul and that they should not hold different opinions. If we each think differently, it is an indication that we are not together in our soul. In such a case, we do not have a co-soul, but an individualistic soul. Therefore, Paul was begging the Philippians to have mercy on him by thinking the same thing and by not having any discord among them. He asked them to think not only the same thing, but even the one thing. Paul expected that all the believers in a locality, no matter how great the number might be, would think the same thing, have the same love, and be together in one soul.

In verses 4 and 5 Paul offers the Philippians the remedy

for their sickness. They suffered from the sickness of not being one in soul. We have the same illness today. I have the assurance that all the saints are one in spirit, but I doubt that we are one in soul. Are you certain that you are one in soul with the other saints? If you are not one in soul, then you are ill just as the Philippians were.

OUR NEED FOR THE BOOK OF PHILIPPIANS

The longer we are in the Lord's recovery, the more we shall learn and the more experiences we shall accumulate. When many of us saw the light regarding the Lord's recovery, we dropped everything of the past and came together to practice the church life. Everything was splendid and wonderful, and we enjoyed a church life honeymoon. After a certain period of time, however, we learned more and accumulated more experiences. Then, out of our learning and experiences, new inventions came forth. Many of us have invented better ways to do things. This causes us to think differently, for every new invention is a different way of thinking. Therefore, because we have a problem in our soul, we need the book of Philippians.

When we came into the church life, we did not have very many opinions. But after staying in the church life for a while, we came to have many opinions. This is not healthy. The remedy for this illness is firstly to take care of the request of the Apostle Paul, who begged that his joy might be made full. To fulfill the joy of the Lord's servant, we need to think the same thing, have the same love, and be together in the soul. Furthermore, we should do nothing through rivalry. When we hold to our various opinions, rivalry is unavoidable. Rivalry comes from the desire to have the preeminence, to be number one. Instead of seeking preeminence for ourselves, we should give it to others. Furthermore, when we are in our opinions, we seek vainglory. Among the Philippians, there was a form of competition. This discord was due to their opinions. What came out of their opinions was rivalry and the seeking of vainglory.

Paul told the Philippians that each man should look not on his own qualities, but also on the qualities of others. Paul was telling them not only to take care of him, but also to take care of the other saints. Then he told them to think that which was also in Christ Jesus. What He thinks we also need to think. Our thinking should be His thinking. This means that in all things we need to be one with Christ. If we cannot be one with Christ in competing with others, we must stop competing with them.

CHRIST AS THE EXAMPLE

Paul goes on to point out Christ as the example. Christ was in the form of God and actually was God Himself. Because He had such a standing, it was not robbery for Him to be equal with God. I believe that as Paul was writing this, deep within he had the feeling that some of the Philippian saints were committing robbery. For example, suppose I do not have the ability to be a leader; nevertheless, I desire to be a leader. In this matter, I rob others of their leadership. Christ, however, did not commit robbery in being equal with God. Although it was not robbery for Christ to be equal with God, He emptied Himself, not insisting on this equality. Furthermore, He humbled Himself, becoming in the likeness of man and taking the form of a slave. This means that Christ gave up His high standing and took not only the form of a man, but the form of a slave. This is an example and pattern for us.

The only way we can follow Christ's example is by the bountiful supply of the Spirit of Jesus Christ. The divine Spirit within us today is the very Spirit of Jesus. When we do things out of rivalry or when we compete with other saints, the Spirit of Jesus is not expressed. But when we take care of the request of the Apostle Paul and look on the qualifications of others, we enjoy the supply of the Spirit of Jesus. By doing this, we spontaneously drop our opinions and are together in one soul.

Many Christian teachers have encouraged others to imitate the pattern revealed in Philippians 2. But it is impossible for us to imitate Christ. For example, we can never be like a lamb. In order to be like a lamb, we need to have the life of a lamb. Likewise, it is impossible for us to imitate the Lord Jesus. The standard of His humility is too high for us. Hallelujah, the Spirit of Jesus is in us! By the Spirit of Jesus we can be just as humble as He was. By the Spirit of Jesus we can fulfill the request of the Apostle Paul and care for all the other saints. By the Spirit of Jesus we can drop all our opinions and be one in spirit and in soul. By the Spirit of Jesus we all can think the one thing and have the same love. This is the testimony of Jesus, the oneness, and the building. This is the practical church, the church lived out of our inner being. This is the Lord's recovery. For this, we need to be one in soul.

If we were one in soul, we would have the genuine enjoyment of Christ. But if there is rivalry and the seeking of vainglory among us, we shall not have any enjoyment of the Lord. Instead, there will be sickness, dryness, and desolation. The Spirit of Jesus, of course, does not want this. In order for us in the church life to experience Christ as our enjoyment, we need to drop our opinions, have one soul, think the same thing, and have the same love.

EXPERIENCING CHRIST FOR THE CHURCH LIFE

The experience of Christ is for the church life. The Christ revealed in chapter two and pursued by Paul in chapter three is not for individual experience, but for the Body life. In Philippians 2 Paul encourages us to think the one thing. This one thing is Christ in our experience for the church life. Although we need to drop our opinions, it is impossible for our mind to be vacant. It needs to be filled with something. If it is not filled with this one thing, something else will fill it. Therefore, we need the vision that God's economy is focused on Christ as our experience for the church life. If our mind is filled with this one thing, there will be no room for other things to come in. Then spontaneously we shall drop our opinions and care for the request of the Apostle Paul and for all the other saints. We shall look not only on the gifts and graces we have received, but also on all the qualities, advantages, and good points of others. Spontaneously, we shall be balanced.

We are accustomed to looking at our own abilities, attributes, and qualifications. The remedy for this is to look at the qualifications of others. A saint once said that if we look at ourselves once, we need to look at Christ ten times. In the same principle, if we look at our ability once, we need to look at the abilities of others five times. This will keep us from extremes. The natural man, however, likes to look on his own work, ability, and qualifications. This causes us to go to an extreme. If we are all at this extreme, what a confusion there will be among us! But if we all look on the good points of others more than on our own good points, we shall be balanced and rescued from extremes. We shall give up our peculiar way of thinking and spontaneously be one in soul with the other saints. In this one soul we not only experience Christ, but also enjoy Him.

To repeat, we need to be not only one in spirit, but also one in soul. Instead of so many different opinions, we should have just one thing about which to think. We should constantly think one thing and have the same love toward everyone. This will rescue our soul from all differences and enable us to be one in soul. If we were all in one soul, thinking the one thing, the situation in the church life would be heavenly. But if we continue to have many different opinions, there will be no enjoyment. Although we may experience Christ, we shall lack the enjoyment of Christ.

Humanly speaking, it is impossible to be one in soul and to think the same thing. But it is easy by the Spirit of Jesus. We do not merely have an outward pattern, for this pattern is in our very being, living Himself out from within us by the Spirit of Jesus. Thus, He is not merely our pattern, but also our life. As He lives Himself out from within us, we can easily drop all our opinions. We all need the vision that Christ, who is the pattern, is within us as life to live Himself out of us. For example, He never insisted upon being anything. Now we have a life within us that never insists on being anything. Rather, this life always humbles Himself, empties Himself, and takes a lower place. Eventually, God the Father exalted Christ to be the highest and gave Him the name that is above every name. Thus, there is no need for rivalry or competition or for the seeking of vainglory. As we enjoy Christ as life within us, eventually God the Father will exalt us and bring us into glory. But there is no need for us to seek even this kind of glory. It depends upon whether or not the Father gives it to us. The most important thing for us to do is to experience Christ as our enjoyment today so that the church may be built up. The building of the church is His glory. Eventually, His glory will become our glory. This is the way for us to be preserved in the Lord's recovery until He comes back.

If we do not take this way, the Lord's recovery will be damaged through our opinions accumulated over the years. This will change the nature of the recovery and cause it to become part of today's Christianity and a continuation of the history of divided and divisive Christianity. May the Lord have mercy upon us to keep us from this. We need to pray, "Lord, keep us and preserve us for Your economy. For the fulfillment of Your purpose, we want to be just like You. We want to have You not only as our pattern, but also as the life that enables us to drop our opinions and to be one in soul with all the saints." If we are like this, the Lord will have the glory, we shall have the enjoyment, and the church will be built up. This is the proper way to enjoy Christ.

Chapter Five

TO THINK THE ONE THING

Philippians 2:12 says, "Wherefore, my beloved, as ye have always obeyed, not as in my presence only, but now much more in my absence, work out your own salvation with fear and trembling." What were the Philippians to obey? They were to obey Paul's word regarding thinking the one thing and being in one soul. The one thing which they were to think is the experience of Christ for the Body life. We may also say that it is the enjoyment of Christ for the Body life. Paul was imploring the Philippians to think this one thing.

THE ONE THING

This one thing is clearly revealed in chapter three, where Paul speaks of the excellency of the knowledge of Christ Jesus the Lord (v. 8). To experience Christ as our enjoyment for the church is excellent. All other things are dung, refuse, dog food. Anything other than this one thing is refuse, food for dogs, not something for us Christians. As children of God, we should not feed on dog food. Rather, we should eat at the table. According to Matthew 15, Christ came as bread for the children of God, not as food for the dogs. However, when the Gentile dogs under the table ate the bread that was for the children of God, the dogs became children of God. Today, we are no longer Gentile dogs, but children of God. The Jews, originally the children of God, have rejected the food and have become dogs. The dogs in Matthew 15 refer to the Gentiles, but, as we shall see, the dogs in Philippians 3 refer to the unbelieving religious Jews. Although the Jews are God's chosen people, they do not eat the food intended for the children of God. Instead, they prefer to eat dog food. Dietitians say that we are what we eat. Thus, spiritually speaking, those who eat dog food become dogs, and the Gentile dogs who eat the food of the children of God become children of God. Through eating we have been metabolically transformed from dogs to the children of God.

Although the Philippians had been transformed from dogs into children of God, at a certain point they turned away to dog food. We can easily do the same thing today. The trash can, the place where the dog food, the refuse, is cast, is primarily in the mind in the case of the brothers and in the emotion in the case of the sisters. Therefore, to think the one thing and to be one in soul eliminates the trash can and all the dog food that is in it. We were reborn as children of God, not in our mind nor in our emotion, but in our spirit. Our dining table is in our spirit. When we get into our spirit, we find ourselves at the dining table where Christ is. The Lord Jesus Christ is our food, and the dining table is in our spirit.

In Philippians 2, Paul was encouraging the Philippians to think the one thing and to be one in soul. The one thing is not merely the objective Christ, but the subjective experience of Christ as our enjoyment for the church life. This one thing should occupy our mind all the time. We should constantly be thinking about how to experience Christ as our rich enjoyment so that we may have the proper church life. The Body life is the issue of the experience and enjoyment of Christ. When we enjoy Christ, the church life spontaneously issues forth. Thus, the church life comes out of our experience of Christ.

We should not only think about this, but even dream about it. Have you ever dreamed of feasting with all the saints at a banquet? Many of us have had dreams like this. Dreams come mainly from impressions, desires, and thoughts. Often, what we dream about is what we have been thinking about or what we desire. We need to think about the experience of Christ and the enjoyment of Christ until we dream about it. This is the one thing that the Apostle Paul charged the Philippians to think about.

ONE IN SOUL

When we all think this one thing, we shall be one in soul.

It is easy for us, the regenerated children of God, to be one in our spirit. As we sing, praise, and pray in the meetings, we are one in spirit. But when the meeting is over, the brothers turn to the mind and the sisters to the emotion. When this happens, we are no longer one. Perhaps in spirit we are still one, but we are not one in soul. The problem with the believers in Philippi was that they were not one in soul. Therefore, Paul charged them to think the one thing and to be one, not in spirit, but in soul. Paul told them that whether he was present or absent, they needed to obey his word. He was asking them to drop all other thoughts and to take his word so that they might think the one thing and be one in soul.

WORKING OUT OUR SALVATION

In Philippians 2:12, Paul tells them to "work out your own salvation with fear and trembling." Since the Philippians were already saved, why did they still need to work out their salvation? When I read this verse as a young man, I was troubled by it and wondered why these saved ones still needed to work out their own salvation. Furthermore, Paul told them to work out their salvation with fear and trembling. When we were saved, we were saved in joy, not in fear and trembling. Thus, the salvation spoken of in this verse is different from eternal salvation. We receive eternal salvation, and there is no need for us to work it out. It has already been accomplished, completed, and presented to us as a gift. But there is another kind of salvation that needs to be worked out. When something is presented to us as a gift, we need only to receive it and enjoy it. Take the example of a dinner that is prepared for you. You do not sit at the dining table eating the food in fear and trembling. No, you enjoy the food. There is another kind of salvation, not for us to receive joyfully, but for us to work out fearfully. Although we have been saved, we still need to be rescued from certain things. As long as you need to be rescued, it proves that you are in a situation that is not positive. You may not be in the big hell, but you may be in a little hell.

MURMURINGS AND REASONINGS

Two of these little hells are seen in verse 14. This verse says, "Do all things without murmurings and reasonings" (Gk.). One little hell is called murmurings, and the other is called reasonings. Murmuring is a hell for the sisters, and reasoning is a hell for the brothers. Murmurings come from the emotion, and reasonings come from the mind. Thus, both the brothers and sisters need to be rescued, the brothers out of their mental hell and the sisters out of their emotional hell. Although we are the saved children of God, we may still fall into the hell of murmuring or into the hell of reasoning. Both our murmurings and our reasonings are little demons. Thus, we need salvation.

The way to be saved from the hells of murmuring and reasoning is to obey the word of the Apostle Paul to think the one thing and to be one in soul. When we think the same thing, we do not murmur or reason. Instead, we experience Christ as our enjoyment. Every part of our mind, emotion, and inner being is filled with the experience and enjoyment of Christ.

Although we have been saved from the eternal hell, we still need to be saved from the small hells of murmuring, complaining, reasoning, and arguing. Every married couple has experienced the exchanging of words. This is a hell. Because the wives murmur and the husbands reason, there are arguments. During the course of such an argument, both the husband and the wife fall into a hell because they are not thinking the one thing. This illustrates how we need to think of the experience and enjoyment of Christ for the church life. If a husband and wife would think one thing, there would be no exchange of words, the wife would be rescued from the hell of the emotion, and the brother would be saved from the hell of the mind. This is a daily, practical, and present salvation. We need to work out this salvation with fear and trembling.

Paul wanted the Philippians to stop their murmurings and reasonings. But how can people stop murmuring or reasoning? It can only be done by turning our thinking to the experience of Christ. Brothers, think this one thing. Sisters, you also think this one thing. If we all think the one thing, there will be no reasonings and murmurings. This is the way to enjoy Christ.

The book of Philippians reveals in detail the way to enjoy Christ. We may consecrate ourselves and follow the inner anointing, but still not have very much of the enjoyment of Christ. However, if we think the one thing, immediately the enjoyment of Christ will be our portion. We all know the doctrine that the proper church life comes out of the experience of Christ. But we may not know the practical way to experience Christ. The wives murmur against their husbands, and the husbands reason with their wives. When we do this, where is the enjoyment of Christ? It disappears. Instead of enjoying Christ, we are in a little hell. As we have seen, the way to be rescued from this hell is to think the one thing. Whenever we do this, we are immediately in the enjoyment of Christ and our family life and church life become very pleasant.

GOD WORKING IN US

Verse 13 says, "For it is God which worketh in you both the willing and the working for his good pleasure" (Gk.). We can work out our own salvation because God works within us. God is mysterious, invisible, and abstract, but He is nonetheless within us. We need to be in fear and trembling lest we miss God, who is our daily salvation. If we miss Him, we miss this practical salvation. It may seem that it is impossible for us to work out our own salvation. If the Philippians had said this, Paul might have replied, "Don't you know that God is working in you? He is working in you both the willing and the working. You may say that you do not have the willingness. But God is working the willingness into you. He is also working in you for the working out of His good pleasure. He works in and you work out. Thus, there is no need for you to do the work by yourself."

Take the example of driving a car. When we drive a car, does the car move us, or do we move the car? We do not have the power to move the car. Thus, it is the car that moves us.

For us to move the car is extremely difficult. But for the car to move us is an enjoyment. If we are out of gasoline, we must move the car. But if we have plenty of gasoline, the car moves us and we enjoy driving. Likewise, as we work out our salvation with fear and trembling, God is working in us both the willing and the working. Because He works in, we can work out. This is like driving a car that is already running. If the car were not running, we could not drive it. In like manner, because God is working within us, we are able to work. Eventually, this is not something fearful; it is an enjoyment. The only reason to be fearful is that we may miss the mysterious, marvelous God within us. We need to care for the indwelling God. If we take care of Him, He will drive the car, that is, He will work in us that we may work out our salvation.

SAVED BY THINKING THE ONE THING

Again I say that we work out our salvation by thinking the one thing. This is the key. We need to think the thing that God is working in us. But when we reason, God stops working. And when He stops, we do not have any enjoyment; rather, we are in a hell. Likewise, our murmuring about things causes God to stop working and puts us into a little hell. The only thing that can cause our reasonings and murmurings to cease is to think the one thing. We need to remember the experience of Christ and to recall how excellent the enjoyment of Christ is. To think this one thing locks the gates of Hades. Even if a brother offends you many times, you need to be occupied with Christ as our enjoyment. Do not care for the brother's offense or allow it to touch you. Rather, have your whole being filled with the thought of the enjoyment of Christ. When our being is filled in this way, we shall have no capacity, energy, or room to think of anything else. If our being is filled with the thought of enjoying Christ, nothing will be able to offend us. Instead of being troubled or offended by others, we shall say, "I am thinking the one thing. Hallelujah for the excellency of the enjoyment of Christ! Hallelujah for the experience of Christ!"

Because God is working in us both the willing and working

for His good pleasure, we can do all things without murmuring or reasoning. If God does not work in us, we shall be murmuring and reasoning all the time. The occupation of the brothers is to reason, and the occupation of the sisters is to murmur. If the brothers do not reason and if the sisters do not murmur, they will all be unemployed. They will be silent. When we think the one thing, everything else is excluded.

BLAMELESS AND HARMLESS

Verse 15 says, "That ye may be blameless and harmless, the sons of God, without rebuke, in the midst of a crooked and perverse generation, among whom ye shine as lights in the world" (Gk.). The word "that" at the beginning of verse 15 indicates a result, an issue. Because we think the one thing and enjoy God's working within us to work out our salvation and do not murmur or reason, we are blameless and harmless. We are like doves, not like scorpions. Murmuring is like the sting of a scorpion. Whenever anyone murmurs, the poison is injected into someone. Such murmuring ones are not harmless. Consider how many people have been stung by their tongue. Through their tongue the poison of death has been spread to many others. Thus, they are not harmless. However, when we think the one thing we are blameless and harmless, for we have the enjoyment of Christ. Then, actually and in a practical way, we behave like children of God without rebuke in the midst of a crooked and perverse generation.

SHINING AS LIGHTS

The first part of verse 16 says, "Holding forth the word of life." In this generation we shine as lights. We do not shine with our own light. Rather, we are illuminators reflecting the light of Christ. The world is a satanic system. In the midst of this organized satanic system, we shine as illuminators holding forth the word of life. There is no need for us to behave. We simply need to think the one thing in order to be full of the enjoyment of Christ. Then we shall be blameless, harmless children of God without rebuke, shining as luminaries in the midst of the satanic system of this perverse and crooked generation. As we shine, we are holding forth the word of life. This is not our conduct or behavior; it is our testimony.

Most of today's Christians are far off the mark. They are taught to behave, to conduct themselves in a certain way. But there is no need for us to behave ourselves, because we are shining as lights and holding forth the word of life. This is not behavior; it is a spontaneous testimony, the living out of the Christ whom we experience and enjoy.

Verse 16 also says, "That I may rejoice in the day of Christ, that I have not run in vain, neither labored in vain." If the Lord's servant can boast in us, then everything is all right. But if he does not feel positively about us, then we are in difficulty.

POURED OUT AS A DRINK OFFERING

Verse 17 says, "But even if I am being poured out as a drink offering upon the sacrifice and service of your faith, I rejoice, and rejoice with you all" (Gk.). In this verse Paul seemed to be saying, "You Philippians are offering something to God. I would like to pour myself out as a drink offering upon your sacrifice." The thought here is quite deep. According to Leviticus, God ordained that His people offer Him daily five main offerings: the burnt offering, the meal offering, the peace offering, the sin offering, and the trespass offering. However, in the first six chapters of Leviticus there is no mention of the drink offering because at that time the children of God did not have the adequate experience of Christ. In other words, at that time Christ was not in them as wine. When you pour yourself out as a drink offering, you need to have a great deal of wine within you. This means that much of Christ has been received into you. The drink offering is not only the objective Christ, like the Christ offered to God in the burnt offering or meal offering, but the subjective Christ who has been taken into us. To pour out the Christ we have experienced is to pour out the wine of the drink offering. As the lamb, Christ could be only the objective burnt offering, not the subjective drink offering. Therefore, Christ must be the wine we drink in so that we may pour Him out as the drink offering.

Paul seemed to be telling the Philippians, "How good it is that you are thinking the one thing and enjoying Christ. This enables you to have something to offer to God as a sacrifice. I would like to pour myself out as a drink offering upon your sacrifice. This means that I would like to pour out the Christ I have experienced upon your experience of Christ." This is what we in the church life need today. All the saints need to think the one thing in order to have the full enjoyment of Christ. Then when they come together, they will be able to offer Christ to God as a sacrifice. Moreover, the church also needs the apostles and the leading ones to have the abundant experience of Christ subjectively to pour out as a drink offering upon the saints' offering. What a rich church life this is! When the children of Israel entered the good land, they had a great deal of wine to drink. Thus, they had the wine to pour out as a drink offering before God. This means that their experience and enjoyment of Christ had become much higher than it was the wilderness. In the church life, we have not only the Christ experienced by the saints and offered to God as offerings, but also upon these offerings the pouring out by the leading ones of the Christ they have experienced. This means that the enjoyment of Christ is poured upon the enjoyment of Christ. This produces a sweet-smelling savor to God. This is the church life that issues out of the full enjoyment of Christ. On the side of the Philippians, it was the sacrifice offered to God. On the side of the Apostle Paul, it was the drink offering. Both are the result of the enjoyment of Christ.

The result of the pouring out of the drink offering upon the offering of the saints is rejoicing. This is the experience of Christ for the church life. The leaders rejoice with the saints, and the saints rejoice with the leaders. We rejoice with one another, and we rejoice together. Because there is rejoicing, there is no murmuring, reasoning, weeping, or suffering. We all need to say, "Lord, recover us to such a high degree. Raise our meetings to such a standard that whenever we come together, many sacrifices will be offered to God and much wine will be poured out by the leaders upon the offerings of the saints." This is possible only by our thinking the one thing and by being one in soul.

OBEYING GOD'S ECONOMY

Recently we have been unjustly accused of being mind benders. We do not bend the mind—we rob it. The church life robs the devilish things from our minds. In the church life we help all the saints to think one thing—the enjoyment of Christ for the church life. We all think of the experience of Christ for the Body life. In doing this, we are obedient.

Whenever we think other things, we are disobedient and rebellious. To think something other than the one thing is to rebel against God's economy. God's economy is that we think the one thing. Has a certain brother offended you? You should not think about that offense, for God's economy does not allow you to do so. If you think about the offense, you rebel against God. This is a serious matter. Murmuring is also rebellious. God's economy does not allow us to murmur. To do so is to be disobedient.

We all have our disposition, and we all are accustomed to murmur, reason, and complain. But if we are enlightened concerning reasoning and murmuring, we shall say, "Lord, forgive my rebellion. I don't want to be a rebel in Your economy. Rather, I want to be obedient, obeying Your economy to think the one thing. Although certain ones have offended me, I do not want to think about the offenses. Instead, I want to think only of the enjoyment and experience of Christ." To do this is to work out our salvation. The salvation in Philippians 2 is actually the proper oneness. To work out our own salvation is to work out this genuine oneness. When we are not in the genuine oneness, we are in some kind of hell. Thus, we need the salvation which is the genuine oneness. We need to be one not only in spirit, but also in soul. As we have said again and again, we need to think the one thing. When we think the one thing, we are one not only in spirit, but also in soul.

Chapter Six

ENJOYING CHRIST BY REPUDIATING THE FLESH

In the past, we have constantly emphasized the spirit. The book of Philippians, however, shows the importance of the soul. As human beings, we are not a spirit or a body, but a soul. Therefore, we Christians must be one not only in spirit, but also in soul. It is very easy to be one in spirit; however, it is difficult to be one in soul, for in the soul we have the troublesome mind, the perplexing emotion, and the stubborn will. In the book of Philippians Paul charges us to be one in soul. The oneness in the soul is the perfect oneness. The oneness in the spirit, on the contrary, is temporary; it cannot last very long. As we pray, sing, and praise the Lord, we are one in spirit. But after we have finished praising, we may find that we are not one in soul. The oneness in the soul is long-lasting. This oneness is found only in Philippians.

The book of Philippians covers the matter of the enjoyment of Christ. This book is unique and contains a number of new and even peculiar expressions. The enjoyment of Christ is in the fellowship in the gospel, in the thinking the one thing, in having the same love, and in the oneness of soul. These are some of the unusual terms found in the book of Philippians.

TWO SYMBOLS

Another unusual term is found in chapter three, verse 2, where Paul says, "Beware of dogs." According to the Bible, a dog is an unclean animal because it does not chew the cud (Lev. 11:26). In order for an animal to be clean, it must chew the cud like a cow or sheep, and it must also have a divided hoof. The hoofs of horses and donkeys are not divided;

therefore, these animals are not clean. But cows and sheep are cloven-footed; hence they are clean. Pigs have a divided hoof, but they do not chew the cud. But dogs neither chew the cud nor are cloven-footed. Both chewing the cud and a divided hoof are symbols in the Bible. A divided hoof signifies discernment in walking, discernment regarding what we should do, where we should go, and the way we should take. If we have a divided hoof, we shall know whether to go to the meeting hall or to the movie theater. But one without a cloven hoof has no discernment regarding his walk. If we do not have the faculty of discernment, we shall become dirty, unclean. To chew the cud is to masticate the words of the Bible. We read the Bible in the way of chewing the cud. For example, by prayreading the words of John 3:16, we chew the cud. If we would chew the words of the Bible, how clean we would become! If we chew the cud and have divided hoofs, we shall be kept from anything defiling. Because we chew the cud and have cloven feet, we are no longer dogs. Rather, we are little lambs.

DOGS, EVIL WORKERS, AND THE CONCISION

Philippians 3:2 says, "Beware of dogs, beware of evil workers, beware of the concision." In the verse Paul exhorts us to beware of three things—dogs, evil workers, and the concision. The fact that there is no conjunction in this verse indicates that these three things refer to one kind of person, a person who is a dog, an evil worker, and part of the concision. The word "evil" in this verse denotes something that is in rebellion against God's economy. According to the Bible, any worker who is against God's regulation is an evil worker. The word concision is a contemptuous term for circumcision. Originally the word circumcision was a term of honor among Jews. But in this Epistle the Apostle Paul used not the word circumcision, but the word concision, a term of despite. In other words, when the Apostle Paul wrote the Epistle to the Philippians, fleshly circumcision was no longer honorable, but dishonorable. Therefore, he used the term concision to diminish the honor of circumcision.

According to the context of this verse, the dogs are the

evil workers, and the evil workers are the concision. Some may wonder how the Jews, who were circumcised according to God's ordination, could become evil workers. The answer lies in the fact that God's dispensation has changed with the coming of Jesus Christ. Before the time of John the Baptist, God ordained that His people be circumcised. That was God's administration, God's economy. But this economy, this dispensation, was terminated by the coming of Jesus Christ. During the present dispensation, God wants people to believe in Jesus Christ, His Son, and to receive Him. This is God's present economy. But the Jews have not abandoned the old dispensation. They prefer the old economy with the law of Moses to believing in Jesus Christ and receiving Him. Therefore, all their intentions in doing things for God are a form of rebellion, for they are rebelling against God's present economy.

It is rebellious to refuse to believe in the Son of God. In God's present economy, He has ordained that His Son should be the object of our faith. God seems to say, "Listen to Him and believe in Him. Do not listen to others." But most of the Jews prefer Moses and the law; they want to remain in the old dispensation. It is not evil to love the law, but the attitude expressed in loving the law when God has changed the dispensation is evil and rebellious.

Under the present dispensation of God, circumcision is not honorable, but dishonorable. Before Him, it is no longer circumcision, but concision. For this reason, Paul tells us to beware of dogs, of evil workers, and of the concision. We must beware of those who practice circumcision in rebellion against God's economy.

THREE POSITIVE ITEMS

We have seen that in verse 2 three matters are mentioned. Verse 3 also mentions three items: worshipping by the Spirit of God, boasting in Christ Jesus, and having no confidence in the flesh (Gk.). These three items are a contrast to the three items found in verse 2. In verse 3 Paul says that we are the circumcision. This means that we, the believers in Christ, are the real circumcision. As the real circumcision, we worship by the Spirit of God. Worshipping by the Spirit of God is in contrast to the dogs. Furthermore, we boast in Christ Jesus. Boasting in Christ is in contrast to the evil workers. Finally, we do not trust in the flesh. Not trusting in the flesh is versus the concision. Because we contact God and worship Him by His Spirit, we are not dogs, and because we are in Christ and boast in Him, we are not rebels or evil workers. Not only have we believed in Christ and received Him, but we are totally in Him. Christ is not only our Savior, but also our life. Hence, instead of being in rebellion, we are in Christ. We are not rebels—we are Christ-men.

We also have no trust in the flesh. The circumcision practiced by the Jews is altogether a matter of the flesh. The Jews trust in the flesh and in what they are in the flesh. We, on the contrary, have no trust whatever in our flesh. The flesh signifies our entire natural being. According to the Bible, the fallen human being is in the flesh. Whether we love or hate, steal or give, we are in the flesh. Do not think that those who rob a bank are in the flesh, but those who donate to charitable organizations are not. The generous ones may be more in the flesh than those who rob, and those who love may be more in the flesh than those who hate. Likewise, those who are humble may be more fleshly than those who are proud. As fallen human beings, we are nothing but flesh. Some people may be very kind, but in the eyes of God, even their kindness is the ugly flesh. Many Christians think of themselves as being capable and intelligent. But whatever comes out of our natural being, whether it be capability or intelligence, is simply the flesh. Therefore, we should not have any confidence in the flesh.

We are those who worship by the Spirit of God, who boast in Christ, and who do not trust in the flesh. We beware of dogs, and we worship by the Spirit of God. We beware of evil workers, and we boast in Christ. We beware of the concision, and we have no trust in the flesh.

ENJOYING CHRIST BY REPUDIATING THE FLESH

The way to enjoy Christ is to repudiate our flesh and our entire natural being. When we reject ourselves in this way, only Christ is left. Then whatever we do will be the experience of Christ. When the unbelievers reject themselves and repudiate their flesh, nothing remains. But when we reject ourselves, we enjoy Christ as the remainder. Christ is what remains after we have rejected our flesh and all we are by nature. This is not merely a doctrine; it is our experience. When the sisters who live together are having problems with one another, perhaps over washing the dishes, they need to reject themselves. When they reject themselves, including their attempt to imitate the pattern of Christ, they will find that Christ remains within them. If a sister washes dishes after doing this, she will have both the experience of Christ and the enjoyment of Christ.

To have no trust in the flesh means to have no trust in ourselves. If we do not trust in ourselves, the self is spontaneously dealt with and Christ is there as the sweet remainder for us to experience. This is the real circumcision because it involves the total rejection of our flesh. The Jews had the form of circumcision but not the reality, which is the cutting off of the flesh. To merely make a mark upon our body actually is not circumcision, but concision. Because we reject our flesh altogether, we are the real circumcision. When the real circumcision takes place, the flesh is gone, and Christ remains. Then whatever we do, say, or think is the enjoyment of Christ.

A CLEAR PICTURE OF THE FLESH

In Philippians 3:4-6 Paul presents a clear picture of the flesh. After saying that he had reason to trust in the flesh, Paul proceeds to list seven aspects of the flesh: being circumcised the eighth day, being of the stock of Israel, being of the tribe of Benjamin, being a Hebrew of the Hebrews, being a Pharisee as concerning the law, being a zealous persecutor of the church, and being blameless according to the righteousness of the law. We may think that the flesh is something bad. These seven items, however, are not bad. Paul was circumcised on the eighth day. Certainly this was very good. He was born of the stock of Israel, not of pagans. Moreover, he was of the tribe of Benjamin, not of Reuben or

Simeon. In the Bible Benjamin is dear, precious, and lovable. Paul was also a Hebrew of the Hebrews. According to the law of God, he was a Pharisee, and according to zeal for God, he persecuted the church. Paul was not indifferent towards God, but loved Him, lived for Him, and even persecuted the church for Him. Finally, according to the righteousness which is in the law, he was blameless. He was perfect, complete, and without defect. Nevertheless, all these items are aspects of the flesh. In fact, they are the constituents of the flesh. Apart from Paul's words in Philippians, we would not consider such things as part of the flesh. But the flesh includes everything natural, whether bad or good. This is the meaning of the flesh in the Bible.

As long as something issues from our natural being, it is of the flesh. If we know this, we are blessed, for we shall not have any trust in ourselves. Rather, we shall reject ourselves utterly. But after we reject ourselves, we shall enjoy Christ as the wonderful, heavenly leftovers. Do not try to adjust yourself. As flesh, we simply cannot be adjusted. Instead of adjusting ourselves, we should repudiate ourselves. If we do this, we shall experience Christ with full enjoyment, enjoying Him in all we do and say.

COUNTING ALL THINGS LOSS AND AS DUNG

After giving us the definition of the flesh in verses 4 through 6, Paul says in verse 7, "But what things were gain to me, those I counted loss on account of Christ" (Gk.). Surely things such as circumcision, being of the stock of Israel, and being of the tribe of Benjamin were a gain to Paul. But if he had kept all these things, there would have been no room in him for Christ. For example, if a bottle is filled with dirt, there is no room for air to get in. First the dirt must be emptied out and then the air will fill it. Likewise, if we still hold on to certain good aspects of the flesh, there will be no room in us for Christ. Therefore, on account of Christ, Paul counted as loss all the aspects of the flesh.

In verse 8 Paul says, "But surely I also count all things loss on account of the excellency of the knowledge of Christ Jesus my Lord, on account of whom I have suffered the loss of all things, and count them dung, that I may gain Christ" (Gk.). Paul seemed to be saying, "I have already counted as loss seven items on account of Christ. Now I also count all things in the whole universe as loss on account of the excellency of the knowledge of Christ." In this universe there is such an excellency as the excellency of the knowledge of Christ Jesus our Lord.

In this verse Paul says that he counts all things dung on account of Christ. According to the usage of the Greek word in ancient times, the word translated dung refers to dog food. It can also be rendered as refuse, garbage, trash. In the eyes of such a seeker after Christ as Paul, everything else was dog food, refuse, trash. The dogs mentioned in verse 2 feed on the dog food spoken of in verse 8. But we feed on Christ, the food of the children of God.

FEEDING ON CHRIST

As we have pointed out, a dog is an unclean person. Now we see that dung is food for unclean people. All the worldly people are unclean, and their food is refuse, trash, dog food. But we, the sons of God, are clean, and our food is Christ. Because He is our food, we need to chew Him, masticate Him, as a cow chews its cud. This is the experience of eating Jesus. Eating is not only a matter of experience, but also a matter of enjoyment. I enjoy every meal I eat. Today we are feasting on Christ. As we feast on Him, we are enjoying Him. The Christ whom we enjoy is what is left over after we have repudiated our flesh. But if we do not reject ourselves and our plans, we shall not have any Christ to eat, for our self and our plans will fill our being and not leave any room for Christ. Therefore, we need to repent and empty ourselves that Christ may have room within us.

The longer we take to eat our food, the more we enjoy it. Likewise, after we reject ourselves, we should enjoy Christ slowly. This is the way to participate in Christ and to feed on Him.

FOUND IN CHRIST

In verse 9 Paul says, "And be found in him." Paul wanted

not only to gain Christ, but also to be absolutely in Christ. He counted all things dung that he might gain Christ and be found in Him. He desired that others would find him in Christ. We also need to be found by one another in Christ. However, suppose you find me angrily rebuking a brother. In such a case you surely would not find me in Christ, but in the flesh. Not only people, but also the angels and demons need to find us in Christ. We should be able to say, "Angels and demons, come and see that I am in Christ. I have gained Christ, and now I am in Christ." This is the experience of Christ.

If we live in Christ, we shall be able to release the riches of Christ in the meetings. In our testimonies the riches of Christ will flow out. If we all experience Christ in this way, what an exhibition of Christ there will be in the meetings! This is the church life. This is what we need today. In the midst of this crooked and perverse generation, God is seeking such a testimony. We are here on earth for this. Our testimony is that we gain Christ and that we are found in Him full of enjoyment.

Chapter Seven

THE EXCELLENCY OF THE KNOWLEDGE OF CHRIST AND THE DETAILED WAY TO EXPERIENCE CHRIST

As we have pointed out, the book of Philippians is on the experience of Christ. It is the only Epistle in the New Testament concerned with the experience of Christ. Although we are familiar with the term the experience of Christ, it is difficult to explain how to experience Him. We have seen that the experience of Christ is mysterious because Christ is mysterious, invisible. Nevertheless, we can experience Him. He is real and can be experienced, yet He is invisible. For this reason, it is difficult to find a verse in the New Testament telling us how to experience Christ. Although the book of Philippians deals with the experience of Christ and although the way to experience Christ is found in this book, the way is a mystery. It is not found on the surface of the book of Philippians. In order to find the way to experience Christ, we need to get into the depths of this book.

In the last message we saw that the way to experience Christ is to repudiate all that we are naturally. All that we have, all that we can do, and all that we are must be rejected and given up. As long as a certain aspect of us is natural, it must be repudiated, no matter how good it may be. Whether our natural constitution is very good or very poor, it must be denied. It takes little effort to deny the worst kind of self, but it requires a great deal of energy to deny the best self. Perhaps you have been treasuring your best self for years. Your friends and relatives all admire it, and you also appreciate it and esteem it highly. Now you hear that you are called upon to repudiate this self in order to experience Christ.

After we repudiate ourselves, we find that something still

remains. This remainder is Christ. As the remainder, Christ is very mysterious. When we cooperate with the mysterious Christ, we not only experience Him, but also enjoy Him. This enjoyment causes us to be happy and excited.

FIVE CRUCIAL MATTERS

In Philippians 3:8 Paul speaks of the excellency of the knowledge of Christ Jesus his Lord. This excellency surpasses the realm of physics, science, and mathematics. In fact, it surpasses everything. I doubt that very many Christians know what the excellency of the knowledge of Christ is.

In Philippians 3 we find the contrast between two kinds of righteousness: the righteousness of the law and the righteousness of God. The righteousness of the law comes from our keeping of the law. For example, the law commands us to honor our parents. If we honor our parents, then this becomes our righteousness according to the law. The law also charges us not to steal. If we refrain from stealing, then we are righteous according to the law in the matter of stealing. The second kind of righteousness seen in Philippians 3 is the righteousness which is of God by faith. Thus, one kind of righteousness is the righteousness of the law, and the other kind of righteousness is the righteousness of God. The law is of dead letters, but God is living. Thus, there is one kind of righteousness which is of dead letters and another kind of righteousness which is of the living God.

In verse 10 Paul speaks of the power of Christ's resurrection and the fellowship of His sufferings. In chapter one there is the fellowship in the gospel and in chapter two, the fellowship of spirit. Here we have the fellowship of Christ's sufferings. In verse 10 Paul also speaks of being conformed to Christ's death. Christ's death is like a mold, and we are like clay pressed into the mold. Eventually, the clay is conformed to the mold. This is a picture of our being conformed to Christ's death. In this message we need to consider these five crucial matters: the excellency of the knowledge of Christ, the righteousness of God by faith, the power of Christ's resurrection, the fellowship of Christ's sufferings, and the conformity to Christ's death.

In verse 11 we find another unusual expression: "the out-resurrection from among the dead" (Gk.). This is not an ordinary resurrection, but an extraordinary resurrection. It refers to something outstanding. This we shall consider in another message.

THE LAW AND CHRIST

In order to know what the excellency of the knowledge of Christ is, we need to see that the main comparison in chapter three is between the law and Christ. Verse 5 says, "According to the law, a Pharisee" (Gk.). Verse 6 says, "According to zeal, persecuting the church; according to the righteousness which is in the law, blameless" (Gk.). In these two verses "according to" is used three times: according to the law, according to zeal, and according to righteousness in the law. In verses 7 and 8 Paul uses the words "on account of" three times: on account of Christ, on account of the excellency of the knowledge of Christ, and on account of whom, referring to Christ. In verse 5 Paul says "according to the law," but in verse 7 he says "on account of Christ." Here we see the contrast between the law and Christ.

A second comparison is that between zeal for the law and the knowledge of Christ. The third comparison is that between the righteousness of the law and the righteousness which is of God by faith. The focal point of these comparisons, however, is the comparison between the law and Christ. The knowledge in verse 8 is not the knowledge of the law, but the knowledge of Christ. This knowledge has its excellency because Christ is excellent.

Do you still believe that the law is excellent? If you say no, I would ask you to compare the law of the Old Testament with the law of the Roman Empire. By this comparison the law of the Old Testament is excellent, for it excels Roman law. But if you compare the Old Testament law with Christ, it does not have any excellence.

THE EXCELLENCY OF THE KNOWLEDGE OF CHRIST

Christ is the embodiment of God. All the fullness of the Godhead is embodied in Christ and dwells in Him. What could be more excellent than the fullness of the Godhead and Christ as the mystery of God? According to the New Testament, no one can know Christ adequately because He is so excellent. In Matthew 11:27 the Lord Jesus said, "No one knows the Son except the Father." Thus, it is impossible for us to know Christ fully; He surpasses all things and far transcends our comprehension. One day, however, the Lord brought His disciples to Caesarea Philippi and asked them to tell Him who people were saying that He was. They said, "Some, John the Baptist; and others, Elijah; and still others, Jeremiah, or one of the prophets" (Matt. 16:14). All these were nonsensical answers. Then the Lord asked His disciples, "But you, who do you say that I am?" (Matt. 16:15). Suddenly Peter responded, "You are the Christ, the Son of the living God" (Matt. 16:16). There is no comparison between the Son of the living God and Elijah or any of the other prophets. After Peter made his declaration regarding Christ, the Lord Jesus said to him, "You are blessed, Simon Bar-jona, because flesh and blood did not reveal this to you, but My Father Who is in the heavens" (Matt. 16:17). The Lord Jesus seemed to be saying, "Simon, you are a son of Jonah, the son of a man of flesh. Nevertheless, you have received a heavenly revelation. This did not come from flesh and blood, but from My Father in the heavens who has revealed it to you. I am not simply a Nazarene, the son of Mary. I am the Son of the living God." With Jesus the Nazarene there was no excellency, but with the Son of the living God there is excellency. None can compare with Him.

Although Peter received the revelation in Matthew 16, in Matthew 17 he acted foolishly on the Mount of Transfiguration. When Moses and Elijah appeared, Peter said, "Lord, it is good for us to be here; if You are willing, I will make three tabernacles here, one for You, and one for Moses, and one for Elijah" (Matt. 17:4). Peter's word offended the heavens. Therefore, a voice from heaven said, "This is My beloved Son, in Whom I delight; hear Him!" (Matt. 17:5). This voice seemed to be saying, "Peter, don't suggest building three tabernacles, one for Moses, one for Elijah, and one for the Lord Jesus. Listen only to the Son of God." This voice was a shock to

THE EXCELLENCY OF THE KNOWLEDGE OF CHRIST

Peter. With the two other disciples, Peter fell on his face. But when they lifted up their eyes, "they saw no one except Jesus Himself alone" (Matt. 17:8). Jesus Christ, the embodiment of the fullness of God, is excellent. His excellence far surpasses that of Moses and Elijah.

When Paul was Saul of Tarsus, he knew nothing of the excellency of Christ. Rather, he thought that the law was marvelous, and, as a Jew, he was proud of it and zealous for it. He appreciated the law to the uttermost. In his zeal for the law, he persecuted the church. One day, on the road to Damascus, a light from heaven suddenly shined upon him, and he was knocked to the ground. At that time he had a vision of Someone more excellent than the law—the Son of the living God. From that time onward, Paul knew that Christ was infinitely superior to the law. The law was given from God and by God, but it was only of dead letters. Now Paul had seen a living Person who was the embodiment of God. Can the law compare to this living Person? Impossible! This living Person may be likened to gold and the law to clay. Before knowing about gold, we may appreciate clay. But by seeing the gold, we receive the excellency of the knowledge of the gold. This illustrates Paul's experience in coming to the excellency of the knowledge of Christ. The excellency of the knowledge of Christ is the excellency of Christ realized by us.

One day a brother brought me a large round stone. This stone was so ugly that I did not care to even touch it. Then the brother said, "Brother Lee, you have said that Christ had no outward beauty or comeliness, but that He was beautiful within. This stone is like Christ in this regard. Outside it is ugly, but inside it is beautiful." Then the brother cut the stone, and within it was a beautiful, transparent crystal. Before he cut the stone, I had no knowledge of the crystal. In fact, I did not appreciate it and wanted to throw it away because it was so ugly. But after the stone was cut, the beauty within appeared before my eyes, and I gained the excellency of the knowledge of the crystal.

In like manner, before his experience on the road to Damascus, Paul did not have the excellency of the knowledge of Christ. Rather, he thought that Jesus was merely an illegitimate son of Mary who was born and raised in Nazareth. Paul treasured the law, but he despised Jesus. But on the road to Damascus, the excellent Jesus appeared to him, and he was shocked when he met the Lord. The Jesus whom Paul thought was buried in a tomb now appeared to him from the heavens. On that day, he learned that Jesus was not earthly, but heavenly and divine. He came to see the excellency of this wonderful One. On account of the excellency of this knowledge of Christ, Paul came to realize that the law cannot compare with Him. Therefore, he could have said, "I have made a comparison between Jesus and the law, and I have decided to take Christ. I count all things loss on account of the excellency of the knowledge of Christ."

Have you ever compared Christ with all other people and all other things? Have you ever compared Him with your degree or with your wife or husband and children? As Christians, we need to make such a comparison. If you compare the sum total of all people and all things with Christ, you will gain the excellency of the knowledge of Christ, and Christ will become all the more dear to you. You will be willing to let go of everything and everyone on account of Christ. Some may think it terrible to count all things loss for Christ. But I am serious in saying that everything must go and that only Christ must remain. When everything has gone, that is the time to experience Christ as the remainder. Christ as the remainder will be incomparably precious and sweet. This is Christ for our experience.

Although the Christ that remains when all other things have been counted loss may seem to be quite small, He is very precious. Whenever I experience Christ and let all other things go, I have the Christ that remains. This remainder may seem quite small, but it is adequate for our appetite.

EXPERIENCING A LITTLE OF CHRIST AT A TIME

When some Christians speak about experiencing Christ, they become greedy and desire to swallow all of Christ at one time. But it took Paul more than thirty years to enjoy Christ. However, some of the young people are impatient in the experience of Christ and complain about enjoying only a little of Him at a time. Do not try to experience too much of Him at once. Simply keep on experiencing Him and enjoying Him daily. Regarding the experience of Christ, we need to slow down and realize that it will take eternity to enjoy Him. Day by day we need to experience a little more of Him. We need to partake of Christ many times a day. In this way we shall have a greater enjoyment of Him. The enjoyment of Christ is an eternal matter. He is inexhaustible, and we cannot exhaust the experience of Him even in a lifetime.

THE RIGHTEOUSNESS WHICH IS OF GOD BY FAITH

Now we come to the second kind of righteousness in Philippians 3, the righteousness which is of God by faith. As we have seen, the righteousness of the law requires us to keep the law. The more we obey the law, the more of the righteousness of the law we shall have. Thus, the righteousness of the law depends upon our effort and behavior. The righteousness of God is different, for it does not depend upon our behavior. Actually, the righteousness of God is simply God Himself living in us and out of us. When God lives in us and then out of us, He becomes our righteousness. For example, it is not we who honor our parents or refrain from stealing. It is the righteous God who lives in us and out of us. By living out of us, He becomes our living righteousness. When we try to keep the law, we endeavor to honor our parents. Even when we are angry, we know that we are obliged to honor our parents and suppress our anger. The righteousness of God by faith is in a different category. God lives in us. This causes us to be full of joy and shining. The righteousness of the law is dead, but the righteousness which is of God Himself is living. We experience this righteousness only when we repudiate ourselves and enjoy Christ as the remainder. At that time, God lives in us and out of us. Then our daily living will be full of God's expression.

THE POWER OF CHRIST'S RESURRECTION

In verse 10 we see that Paul wanted to know the power of Christ's resurrection. This power is the resurrected Christ living in us. Our Christ today is the resurrected One. As the resurrection, He lives within us. Like a dynamo, the resurrected Christ lives within us as our source of power. When we repudiate our flesh and our natural man, we often have a sense of this power working in us. Christ as the remainder is like a motor empowering us from within. This is the power of His resurrection.

Because we have the power of resurrection, it is easy to die with Christ. The second stanza of a hymn written by A. B. Simpson goes like this:

> 'Tis not hard to die with Christ
> When His risen life we know;
> 'Tis not hard to share His suff'rings
> When our hearts with joy o'erflow.
> In His resurrection power
> He has come to dwell in me,
> And my heart is gladly going
> All the way to Calvary.

A. B. Simpson certainly knew Christ as resurrection power. He knew that the resurrected Christ lived in him as resurrection power. By this resurrection power, we can overcome all negative things, including Satan himself. The Christian life is a life lived by resurrection power. Experiencing the power of Christ's resurrection requires that we repudiate the flesh, the self, and the natural man. When we do this, we shall experience the resurrection power within. By this power we experience all the riches of Christ.

THE FELLOWSHIP OF CHRIST'S SUFFERINGS

Now we come to the fellowship of Christ's sufferings. The sufferings here are different from our common sufferings. Most of our sufferings are not Christ's sufferings. To know the fellowship of Christ's sufferings, we must know the difference between Christ's sufferings and our common sufferings. Christ's sufferings were for the fulfillment of God's purpose. Christ did not suffer for any other reason. We, on the contrary, suffer not because we are fulfilling God's will, but because we have made so many mistakes. Suppose, for example, a certain brother is quite lazy. By oversleeping in the morning, he misses the bus for school. Because he is late for school, he suffers discipline at school upon his arrival. Such suffering is not the suffering of Christ. It is the suffering that comes upon us because of our mistakes.

We need to be clear what the sufferings of Christ are. Suppose a brother who is a student has a genuine, living testimony at school. This testimony causes him to be persecuted for the sake of Christ. This persecution is the suffering of Christ. To remain in this kind of suffering is to share in the fellowship of Christ's suffering for the fulfillment of God's purpose. The suffering that comes from being persecuted for bearing a living testimony to the Lord is in the same category as Christ's suffering for the fulfillment of God's purpose. We all must stay in this kind of suffering. This is the fellowship of His sufferings.

Whenever you repudiate your flesh and your self, you will experience Christ and enjoy Him. But due to your enjoyment of Christ, opposition will come to you, and you will suffer persecution. You will be persecuted because the world today is against God's economy and the testimony of Jesus. When you suffer opposition and persecution, you share in the fellowship of Christ's suffering.

BEING CONFORMED TO CHRIST'S DEATH

In this verse Paul also speaks of being conformed to Christ's death. Christ's humanity was like a shell, and He as the embodiment of God was concealed and confined within this shell. Outwardly He had no glory, but inwardly He was filled with the glory of God. How could the glory within shine out? The only way was by death. Christ's death was the breaking of the outer shell of His humanity. Through His death, His human shell was broken, and the divine glory was released. In other words, His death broke His humanity and released His divinity.

As human beings, we also have our humanity as a shell. Our shell, of course, is not pure, as Christ's was. Because we have been born again, the divine life is in us. However, it is concealed within this shell of our humanity. Therefore, we need to experience the kind of death that breaks the shell of our humanity and releases the glory of the divine life within us. For this to take place, we need to be conformed to Christ's death. Christ's death is the death that breaks the human shell and releases the divine glory. We need such a death day by day.

Whenever we repudiate our flesh and all that we are by nature, Christ remains within as our enjoyment. As we enjoy Christ, we must be prepared to experience the death that breaks our natural man. From this kind of death there is no escape. The death of Adam is terrible, but the death of Christ is lovely. Hence, we all must love the death of Christ and be willing to be conformed to it.

Each day as I experience Christ, the experience of Christ brings me into a situation of death. This death situation, however, is lovable and not dreadful. Even God loves the death of Christ. This situation of death may involve our wife or husband or the elders in the church. By experiencing this death, the natural man that we have already repudiated and set aside is killed. At times Christ may seem to say, "Since you have repudiated your flesh, let Me kill it." This killing is the conformity to the death of Christ. Eventually, we shall be fully conformed to Christ's death. At that time, others will be able to see in us and upon us the working of death that kills our flesh, self, and natural man. This death breaks the outer shell and releases the inward glory.

All of the five points covered in this message are part of the detailed way to experience Christ. If we experience these five items, we shall one day attain to the out-resurrection from among the dead. We shall cover this matter in a later message.

CHAPTER EIGHT

ENJOYING CHRIST BY COUNTING ALL THINGS LOSS

In the previous message we saw five crucial items in Philippians 3: the excellency of the knowledge of Christ, the righteousness which is of God by faith, the power of Christ's resurrection, the fellowship of Christ's sufferings, and the conformity to Christ's death. These five matters relate to one concept—living by Christ that we may obtain Him. The word "obtain" in Philippians 3:12 (Gk.) implies the experience of Christ and the enjoyment of Christ. To obtain Christ means to lay hold of Him, or to gain possession of Him. Christ is everything to us, our portion, our destiny, and even our destination. Now we must lay hold of Him and take possession of Him.

This is similar to the way the children of Israel took possession of the good land. The land had been destined for them and assigned to them, but they had to take possession of it little by little. The more they took possession of the land, the more they obtained the land; and the more they experienced the land, the more they enjoyed the land. The land is a complete type of the all-inclusive Christ. As our portion, Christ has been assigned to us. But now we need to take Him, to gain Him, to obtain Him.

GAINING CHRIST

In verse 8 Paul says, "That I may gain Christ" (Gk.). According to the Greek, in verse 12 Paul speaks of obtaining that for which he had been obtained of Christ Jesus. The Greek word for obtain is used in two ways here: the first refers to obtaining in an ordinary way and the second to obtaining in an intensified way. This means that we must not only obtain Christ, but that our obtaining of Him must be intensified.

THE EXCELLENCY OF THE KNOWLEDGE OF CHRIST

The best way to obtain Christ is to experience Him. We need to consider how to experience Christ and enjoy Christ in a practical way. As we have pointed out, in verse 8 Paul speaks of the excellency of the knowledge of Christ Jesus. Before Christ came, the children of Israel were God's people on earth. They were the only people who had received something directly from God. What they received from God directly was the law. This was a great matter, and the Jews were proud of the law and boasted in it. The law was their glory and excellency. Unlike the Jews, the Gentiles could not boast of having received anything directly from God. But the Jews could say, "All the nations are dogs, but we are the chosen people of God, the peculiar possession of God. We have the law of God." No one can say that the law is not good. However, about fifteen hundred years after the law was given, Jesus of Nazareth appeared. Although He had no beauty or comeliness, He came to certain people and said, "Follow Me." This word implied that those who followed Him had to forget the law. The words, "Follow Me," caused a great disturbance. Some might have said, "We have been following Moses for centuries. Who are you, a Nazarene, to tell us to follow you?" Nevertheless, some young fishermen named Peter, Andrew, James, and John left their boats and their nets and followed Jesus. Jesus was a powerful magnet who attracted them to Himself. Those who followed Him were not Pharisees, scribes, or Sadducees, but uneducated fishermen. Those who followed Him were not the leaders in Jewish society.

One day the Lord Jesus brought His disciples to Caesarea Philippi and asked them who people were saying that He was. They told Him that some said that He was Elijah, Jeremiah, John the Baptist, or one of the prophets. But when He asked them who they thought He was, Peter immediately replied, "You are the Christ, the Son of the living God." This means that Jesus, the Nazarene, was the Christ, the Messiah, God's anointed and appointed One. Peter seemed to be saying,

"You, Jesus of Nazareth, are the anointed and appointed One of God. You are also the Son of the living God."

After Peter declared that Jesus was the Christ, the Son of the living God, the Lord Jesus told His disciples that He would be crucified and resurrected on the third day. But the Lord's followers could not believe it. They could recognize Him as the Christ, the Son of the living God, but they could not believe that He would be crucified and resurrected. Eventually, the Lord was betrayed, arrested, judged, and crucified. The disciples were very disappointed because the Son of the living God had been killed and buried. But on the third day He was resurrected. The resurrection was discovered not by Peter, but by a sister who loved the Lord. She saw the empty tomb and even touched the resurrected Christ. Then the Lord charged her to tell the disciples that He would meet them in Galilee. Thus, after Christ's resurrection all the disciples came to know the excellency of Christ Jesus the Lord.

But many of the "top dogs" among the Jews did not know this excellent One. One of these "top dogs" was a young man named Saul of Tarsus. Saul appreciated the law to the uttermost, and he tried his best to damage the churches. But one day the excellent Jesus appeared to him from the heavens in a mysterious way, even calling him by name. Saul saw the light and heard the voice, but he did not see anyone. How shocked Saul was to discover that the One speaking to him was Jesus! To his concept, Jesus was in the tomb. But now he heard Jesus speaking to him from the heavens. At that time, the veil was removed, and Saul of Tarsus had a vision of the Lord Jesus. This vision gave him the excellency of the knowledge of Christ.

For the excellency of the knowledge of Christ, Paul became willing to drop everything. He realized that there was no comparison between Christ and the law. How could the ten commandments compare with this living, wonderful Person? All the things that had been gain to Paul he now counted as loss for the excellency of Christ.

GAINING CHRIST BY EATING HIM

Paul also desired to gain Christ, to obtain Him, to take

possession of Him. The best way to take possession of something is to eat it. Dietitians say that we are what we eat. Therefore, by eating Christ, Christ gets into us and then comes out of us. When Christ comes into us, He is our life supply. But when He comes out of us, He is the righteousness which is of God by faith. When we eat Christ, He becomes the life supply within us. Then this Christ will live Himself out of us. When He does this, He becomes our living righteousness. This is the righteousness of God.

Furthermore, when we take Christ into us by eating Him, Christ becomes the resurrected One within us. In this resurrected One there is the power of resurrection that motivates us and energizes us. Because we are energized by resurrection power, we cannot be silent. Rather, we must be excited and even beside ourselves with joy. This is the power of resurrection. This is Christ, not in doctrine, but in our experience.

A PARTICULAR WAY TO EAT CHRIST

Although the food has been prepared and set on the table, we may not know how to eat. In Philippians 3 we see a very particular way to eat Christ. The best way to eat Him is by denying something. In order to eat Christ, we must deny everything, including ourselves, our mind, our cleverness, our knowledge, and all our good points. We must even deny yesterday's experience of Christ. Paul said that he counted all things loss on account of the excellency of the knowledge of Christ. This means that he denied everything. Because Christ was everything to him, he denied everything other than Christ.

A certain person may be humble, and another may be very bold. The humble one has been humble from birth. There is no need to teach him to be humble. He simply does not know that there is any such thing as pride. The bold one was born with the ability to release his spirit. It is natural for him to do so. However, for the humble one to release his spirit is difficult, and for the bold one to be humble is a killing to him. A third person may naturally be very intelligent. He was born that way. Humility, boldness, and intelligence are the heritage these persons have from birth. A fourth person may be very kind and gentle. One day all four may come to believe in the Lord Jesus and become partakers of Christ. Suppose a servant of the Lord visits them and tells them that our only destiny is to obtain Christ. In order to gain Christ, we must count all things loss. However, the humble brother may count all things loss except his humility. In principle, the same may be true of the bold brother, the intelligent brother, and the gentle brother. Because the humble brother has not counted his humility as loss for the sake of Christ, he will use his humility in the church life whenever an opportunity is presented. Although he is humble, there is nothing of Christ in his humility. He secretly treasures his humility and thus it replaces Christ. The same is true regarding natural boldness, natural intelligence, and natural gentleness. All these things are simply aspects of the flesh.

If we want to participate in Christ, experience Christ, and enjoy Christ, we must repudiate our flesh. The greatest obstacle to enjoying Christ is our natural heritage. For example, the greatest hindrance for a naturally gentle brother to enjoy Christ is his gentleness, for he may repudiate all things except his gentleness. Although we have enjoyed Christ to a certain degree, we all have been frustrated and hindered by our natural heritage. It is the good flesh that is the greatest hindrance to experiencing Christ and enjoying Him.

Suppose a certain person is naturally eloquent and makes a great impact upon an audience. If he becomes a Christian, he can be an outstanding preacher and draw a great crowd. Being naturally eloquent, he can be influential and have a great impact. But there will be no need for Christ or for the Spirit. With his natural eloquence, he can secure a large following. If I were such an eloquent speaker, you all would appreciate me. You would praise the Lord that such a brother had been brought into the Lord's recovery. However, it is difficult for such an eloquent speaker to enjoy Christ in his speaking because he has no need of Christ.

Suppose another person is not born with the ability to speak eloquently. On the contrary, he is slow and halting in his expression. Whenever he speaks more than a few minutes, everyone falls asleep. Suppose he gets saved, loves the Lord and the church, and has a burden to speak a word for the Lord. Having no trust in himself, he spontaneously repudiates himself and puts all his trust in Christ. He may fast and pray desperately to the Lord, saying, "Lord, if You don't speak, I will not be able to speak. If You don't do something with my speaking, I am finished." When he stands up to speak, he is in fear and trembling. But because he has repudiated himself, he experiences Christ and enjoys Christ as he speaks.

A naturally eloquent brother may have the same experience, for with him the principle is the same. He may pray, "Lord, I am in fear and trembling that my eloquence and intelligence might replace You and that my ability might hinder You and keep me from enjoying You. Lord, as I speak I have no trust in my natural ability." In this way he denies himself and repudiates his ability, eloquence, intelligence, and knowledge. Therefore, when he speaks, he also experiences Christ and enjoys Him.

No matter whether we are dull or intelligent, we must reject all that we are. Nothing natural should be allowed to replace Christ. Any naturally good thing will frustrate us from the enjoyment of Christ.

OBTAINING THAT FOR WHICH WE HAVE BEEN OBTAINED

The Apostle Paul said, "I pursue, if also I may obtain that for which I have been obtained by Christ Jesus" (v. 12, Gk.). Christ has obtained us that we may obtain Him. One day we repented and believed in Christ. According to our feeling, we were saved, but according to Christ's realization, we were captured by Him. Christ has taken possession of us, not that we may go to heaven or be good Christians, but that we may obtain Him. We need to pursue Him so that we may lay hold of that for which we have been laid hold of by Him. Therefore, we should say, "Lord, I thank You for obtaining me. You have obtained me so that I may obtain You. This was Your purpose in taking possession of me."

As we have pointed out, the best way to obtain Christ is to eat Him. He desires that we eat more and more of Him. In order to eat Christ, we must deny whatever we are, whatever we have, and whatever we are able to do. This is the way to obtain that for which we have been obtained by Christ.

It is not simply a matter of learning Christ, but of taking possession of Him. By denying all that we are naturally, we take possession of Him. We must deny not only our hatred, but also our love; not only our pride, but also our humility; not only our dullness, but also our intelligence. The way to enjoy Christ is to deny everything that we are by nature.

COUNTING ALL THINGS LOSS

According to Philippians 3, to deny everything is to count everything loss because of Christ, because of the excellency of the knowledge of Christ. How excellent Christ is! This excellent knowledge will motivate us to count all things loss. We must even deny our knowledge of the Bible. I have been studying the Bible for more than fifty years, and I have acquired a good deal of Bible knowledge. However, if I trust in my knowledge while I am giving a message, that message will amount to nothing. Every time I speak I have learned to say to the Lord, "Lord, I have nothing. Even if I have something, it does not count. Lord, You must come in to be everything. Lord, You be the speaking, the outline, the points, the instant utterance, and the whole message." When I speak like this, something new is released time after time, and I am the first one to be fed. However, if I trust in my knowledge, even the knowledge I received yesterday, I shall not have any nourishment. In such a case, I would be trusting in something good that is not Christ.

Again I say, the way for us to enjoy Christ is to deny everything we have and are. We must even deny the best spiritual experiences we have had. The way to eat Christ is to deny everything and to come to Him empty-handed. If you empty out your whole being, He will be something new to you.

Paul not only counted all things loss for the sake of Christ, but counted all things as dung. According to his accounting, everything meant nothing. Because he always counted everything loss for the sake of Christ, he constantly enjoyed Christ.

The more things you deny, the more Christ will replace you and the more He becomes your experience and enjoyment. Our slogan should be this: "Oh, that I may gain Christ!" Oh, that we may also obtain that for which we have been obtained by Christ. The way to obtain Him, gain Him, experience Him, and enjoy Him is to deny whatever we are, whatever we have, and whatever we can do. Do not bring anything to Christ. He does not need what you are or have, but you need Him. In every way Christ wants to replace you with Himself. Christ has already obtained us that we may obtain Him. Now He is waiting for us to experience Him and enjoy Him by denying all things and by counting all things loss for His sake.

Chapter Nine

ATTAINING THE OUT-RESURRECTION BY BEING FILLED WITH CHRIST

In the book of Philippians Paul uses certain unusual expressions that are not found elsewhere in the Bible. Some of these expressions are "the excellency of the knowledge of Christ," "the power of His resurrection," "the fellowship of His sufferings," and "being conformed to His death." Although these expressions may be familiar to us, we may not understand them adequately. In this message we shall consider another peculiar expression, "the out-resurrection." This refers to the resurrection that is outstanding, not the ordinary resurrection. This resurrection is like graduation with highest honors. Hundreds of students may graduate at the same time, but only one is the valedictorian, one whose graduation is outstanding. We may call this kind of graduation the outstanding-graduation, or the extra-graduation. When Paul wrote this Epistle, he probably realized that he would soon be martyred. Believing that there would be a resurrection at the time of the Lord's coming back, he was assured that he would participate in the resurrection. However, he desired to attain to the out-resurrection from among the dead, the outstanding resurrection.

PAUL'S DESPERATION

In Philippians 3:11 Paul says, "If by any means I might attain unto the out-resurrection from among the dead" (Gk.). The words "by any means" reveal that Paul was desperate. He was like a runner in a race who is desperate to be first. Paul's concept was that of a race in the Olympic games. By any means, he wanted to arrive at the goal of the out-resurrection.

We all need to have this sense of desperation infused into us. We need to be desperate to attain the out-resurrection.

FILLED WITH CHRIST

A student becomes valedictorian by doing outstanding work in his studies and by being filled with all he has learned. In order to be valedictorian, you must be the graduate most filled with learning. Likewise, in order for Paul to attain to the out-resurrection from among the dead, he had to be filled with Christ. Today, many young people are good at shouting and releasing the spirit. However, when the Lord Jesus comes back, what will count is how much we have been filled with Christ. It is possible to shout and release the spirit and yet be short of Christ. There is nothing wrong with shouting and releasing the spirit. But inwardly we need to be filled with Christ. When the Lord Jesus comes back, He will be concerned with the degree to which we have been filled with Him, not with how much shouting we have done. How much Christ have you obtained? How much Christ has filled your being? If you are filled with Christ, then you will be qualified for the out-resurrection.

We should not only shout in the meetings, but be filled with Christ and express Christ in our daily living. God does not want shouting or release. He wants His Son, Jesus Christ, to be wrought into our being to become our life and our living. Christ must be our everything. The more we receive of Christ, the more qualified we shall be to attain to the out-resurrection from among the dead.

Paul's concept in Philippians 3 is that of gaining and obtaining Christ. As I have pointed out, the word obtain implies both experience and enjoyment. Thus, Paul wanted to experience Christ and enjoy Christ. This means he desired to participate in Christ, to partake of Christ, and to have Christ wrought into the fibers of his being.

STRETCHING FORTH TO CHRIST

In verses 13 and 14 Paul said, "One thing I do, forgetting those things behind, and stretching forth unto those things before, I pursue toward the goal for the prize of the above calling of God in Christ Jesus" (Gk.). Paul was stretching forth to Christ. In order to understand Paul's meaning here, we need to realize that every age has a trend, a current, a tide. The trend of the age is always versus Christ. There are many things in the current of the age that can carry us away from Christ. Christ leads us upward to the heavens, but the current of the age leads us downward. Everything during Paul's time, including Judaism, Greek philosophy, Gnosticism, and Roman politics, was versus Christ. It is not easy to move upward when there is such a strong current to pull us downward. Therefore, like Paul, we need to be desperate to move against the current of the age.

Paul was desperate to stretch forth upward to Christ. In the Lord's recovery we also need to fight against the downward trend. Satan is subtle, and he can use anything as a substitute for Christ. He can even use pray-reading, praising, or the release of the spirit to replace Christ. Satan's intention is simply to keep us away from Christ. If he can accomplish this, he is satisfied. As long as we do not obtain Christ, Satan is happy with our shouting, calling, and pray-reading. Thus, in all our activities we need to check whether or not we are obtaining Christ. Do we obtain Christ in our release of the spirit, in our pray-reading, or in our meetings? The test, the standard, is the gaining of Christ. It is not calling, shouting, or releasing the spirit. We need to be assured that in whatever we do we are gaining more of Christ. The growth of life is simply the increase of Christ. It is the daily addition of Christ into our being.

Do not think that I am now opposed to shouting, calling on the name of the Lord, or pray-reading the Word. I took the lead to practice these things. I even encouraged others to make a joyful noise in the presence of the Lord. But I wish to point out that merely calling, shouting, pray-reading, or releasing the spirit without Christ is an offense to God. Again and again we have pointed out that to be religious is to do something to please God without Christ. If you shout, release the spirit, or pray-read without Christ, that is religion. It may be a new religion, a religion invented by us, but it is nonetheless a religion, for we are trying to please God without Christ. To do these things is to be carried downward away from Christ. To receive Christ is to move upward, but to miss Christ is to be carried downward. If you desire to shout, you must check how much of Christ there is in your shouting. If you do not have the assurance that Christ is in your shouting, you should be quiet. The same is true with the release of the spirit and with the calling on the name of the Lord. Anything we do to worship God without Christ is religious. Like Paul, we need to be desperate to obtain Christ.

By the time Paul wrote the Epistle to the Philippians, he was matured. Nevertheless, he was still hungry to obtain Christ and experience Him. He had no assurance that he had already attained. Thus, he said that he was forgetting the things behind and stretching forward to the things before. He wanted to set aside everything of the past, whether it was good or bad. Both his Jewish experiences and his Christian experiences had to be left behind that he might obtain Christ. Paul seemed to be saying, "Not only my attainments in Judaism can frustrate me from seeking Christ, but even my experiences in the churches can do this. Anything old can keep me from experiencing Christ today. Therefore, I am forgetting the things behind and stretching forth to the things before. Every aspect of the things before is just Christ Himself."

In Philippians 3:14 Paul said, "I pursue toward the goal for the prize of the above calling of God in Christ Jesus." The Greek word for "pursue" is of the same root as the word for "persecute." Anyone who persecutes others is desperate. Paul was desperate to follow after Christ and to seek Christ. We all need such a desperation.

THE TESTIMONY OF JESUS CHRIST

The meetings of the church should be a testimony of our daily living and our daily walk. What is the testimony of our meetings? What do the visitors see when they come to the meetings? Do they simply see us shouting, pray-reading, and calling on the name of the Lord? In our meetings we need to have some genuine testimonies of our experience of Christ and enjoyment of Christ. Thus, whenever the visitors come to our meetings and observe what is taking place, they will be convinced that this is the testimony of Jesus Christ. My present concern for all the churches is that we would have the experience of Christ. If people can see only our shouting and excitement, then we must be short of Christ. If so, we have lost the Lord's testimony. In the meetings we must have something real, solid, practical, convincing, and subduing. The visitors need to be impressed with the riches of Christ. Whenever a visitor comes to the meeting, he should be convinced and subdued and say, "Here is the testimony of Jesus. This is not just a group of people shouting, singing, and praising, for the reality of Christ as life is among them. In their testimonies they all tell of how they are experiencing Christ in their daily life. Thus, when they come together they have much of Christ to present to God." If we are like this, our meetings will be the exhibition of Christ. What God desires today is such a testimony of Jesus.

PAUL'S GOAL

In Philippians 3 Paul did not think that he had yet reached the goal. Thus, he pursued Christ by forgetting the things past and stretching forth to the things before. Paul's goal was the top experience of Christ, the fullest portion of Christ. Our goal in the church life should be the best experience of Christ. If we reach this goal, we shall be filled with Christ. Then we shall receive the reward of the out-resurrection from among the dead. Because we are outstanding in the experience of Christ and are filled with Christ to the uttermost, we receive the reward of the out-resurrection. This is the accurate meaning of this portion of the Word.

THINKING ONE THING

Verse 15 says, "Let us therefore, as many as are full-grown, think this: and if anything otherwise ye think, God shall reveal also this unto you" (Gk.). In chapter two Paul charged the Philippians to think the one thing. The one thing we need to think is forgetting everything of the past and stretching forth to pursue the goal of the best experience of Christ that we may receive the prize. Let us all think this one thing. We need to be occupied with how to be filled with Christ and how to take the lead in the experience of Christ.

In this verse Paul says also, "If anything otherwise ye think, God shall reveal also this unto you." This indicates that it is quite possible for us to think something else. If we do, God will reveal even this to us. We may be willing to let go of the one thing, but God is not willing. We may forget about the experience of Christ and become occupied with things such as shouting and releasing the spirit. We may even compete with others in these matters. However, we need to be like Paul to pursue the goal of the experience of Christ and the enjoyment of Christ. We do not want to talk about Christ without having the experience of Christ. However, we may turn from pursuing Christ and seek to have our own way regarding certain things in the church life. When we do this, we have no joy within us. When we are like this, we are in the flesh, and we are not experiencing Christ. The mysterious Christ seems to disappear.

If we exercise our mentality instead of our spirit, we shall not experience Christ. If we argue with one another and compete with one another, we do not experience Christ because we are not in our spirit. We need to have Christ not in terminology, but as a reality. We need to be centered not on things, but on Christ Himself. We all need to see the vision that what the Lord desires today is Christ. If we learn this lesson, we shall not care for our way or our success. Rather, we shall say, "Lord, we are here to gain You. Show us the way to gain You more. We don't want to simply have meetings. We want to have You. We have been obtained by You so that we may obtain You. Lord, what is the way for the saints in this locality to experience and enjoy You more?" This is the right attitude to have before the Lord.

What the Lord desires today is not simply meetings, work, or activities. Furthermore, He does not desire any practices. What He wants is for us to be living and full of Christ. Then whatever we do and are will be the living testimony of Jesus Christ. This is what the Lord needs today.

WALKING BY THE SAME RULE

In verse 16 Paul says, "Only this: whereto we have attained, let us walk by the same rule" (Gk.). No matter the degree of our experience, we need to walk by the same rule. This rule is to think the one thing. Do not say, "Brother Lee, you have been in the Lord for more than fifty years and have a great deal of experience. You are matured and on a high level. But we have been in the church life a short time." No matter on what level we are, we need to walk by the same rule and to think of nothing other than the experience of Christ for the church life. To walk by the same rule is simply to think the one thing. For this reason, Paul besought Euodias and Syntyche to think the same thing (4:2). No matter what our age may be, young, middle-aged, or elderly, and no matter how long we have been in the church life, we need to walk by the same rule by thinking the one thing. If we do this, the situation in the church life will be wonderful. By thinking the one thing we shall be kept in oneness and in life. Instead of divisions or opinions among us, there will be the genuine oneness with life.

Throughout the recovery, we all need to think the one thing—to pursue Christ toward the goal for the prize. If we do this, we shall be in oneness, and we shall be full of life. This is my burden in these days. I hope that you all will be infused with this burden and from now on will not care for anything other than the best enjoyment of Christ. We all want to be filled with Christ so that we may attain to the outstanding resurrection, the out-resurrection from among the dead. We want to think the one thing so that we may be one not only in spirit, but also in soul. Furthermore, by thinking the one thing, the reality of the riches of Christ will reach its fullness. This is the Lord's recovery.

Chapter Ten

IN HIM—THE SECRET OF EXPERIENCING CHRIST

As we have pointed out, in the book of Philippians Paul uses a number of unusual expressions. One of these expressions is found in chapter four, verse 12. Here Paul says, "In everything and in all things I have learned the secret" (ASV). The phrase "learned the secret" indicates that Paul had come into a new situation, a new environment. Whenever we are put in a new environment, we need to learn the secret of living in that environment. For someone from the West to go to the Far East is for him to go into a new environment. In order to live, he must learn the secret of life there. For example, when brothers and sisters from the United States visit the Far East, they need to learn the secret of eating with chopsticks. If they do not learn the secret, they will not be able to eat.

PAUL'S SECRET—BEING IN CHRIST

In Philippians 4:12 Paul says, "I know both how to be abased, and I know how to abound: every where and in all things I have learned the secret both to be full and to be hungry, both to abound and to suffer need." Here Paul seems to be saying, "In all things I have been instructed with the secret so that I know how to be in want and how to abound. I have been initiated with a type of secret knowledge." What is the secret Paul learned? Because Paul had been instructed with the particular secret, he could handle any situation, whether he was rich or poor, filled or hungry. The secret is in Philippians 4:13: "I can do all things in Him who empowers me" (Gk.). The secret is not that Christ is in us; it is that we are in Him.

Most of us do not know how to apply the fact that we are in Christ. Take riding in a car to the meeting as an example. My secret in coming to the meeting is simply to sit in the car and to let someone else drive. What a problem it would be if I refused to get into the car or did not like being in the car and did certain foolish things to get out of the car! On the day we were saved, God put us into the heavenly car, the best car in the universe. The name of this car is Christ. On the day we were saved, we were put into Him. If we would exercise to be in Him in a practical way, we would not be active to do so many things on our own. Instead, we would simply rest and be at peace. If we are in Christ, we shall be at rest and not endeavor to overcome negative things such as our temper. Although we were put into Christ on the day we were saved, to the feeling of many Christians they are not yet in Christ.

ENJOYING SALVATION BY BEING IN CHRIST

I appreciate the fact that Christ lives in us. There is even a hymn in our hymnal with this chorus:

> Christ liveth in me,
> Christ liveth in me;
> Oh! what a salvation this,
> That Christ liveth in me.

However, simply to say that Christ lives in us is to be too objective. We also need to experience living in Christ and doing all things in Him. What a salvation it is to live in Him! If we live in Him, we shall enjoy His salvation day by day. This salvation can be compared to riding in a car. As long as we remain in the car, we enjoy salvation. When I ride in a car, I am not worried about what direction I am going or anything else. I may rest, pray, or enjoy sight-seeing. I simply rest and enjoy myself. In like manner, when we are in Christ, we should simply rest and enjoy ourselves. We should enjoy the life in Christ.

My burden in this message is that we would all learn the secret of being in Him. We can do all things in Him. This may seem to be a small secret, but actually it has great

IN HIM—THE SECRET OF EXPERIENCING CHRIST

significance. This secret is the way for us to experience Christ and to enjoy Christ. It is also the secret of having more of Christ accumulated within us.

PRACTICING THE SECRET

Such a secret needs to be put into practice. In order to practice this secret, we firstly need to realize that Christ lives in us. Secondly, we must deny the flesh and the natural man. We should count all things loss and not treasure or appreciate anything of our natural man, such as our humility or other virtues. All of our good points, attributes, and virtues need to be counted loss. We should not have any confidence in anything other than Christ. Thirdly, we should not do anything by ourselves, for we are not alone. Another person lives in us.

Marriage is an illustration of this. Before we were married, we were alone. If we wanted to open the window, we simply opened it. But when we were married, we became bound and limited. All the wives are tied to their husbands, and all the husbands are tied to their wives. In my married life I certainly have learned to live by another person, by my wife. With Christ, we have another person, not married to us, but living in us. However, many of us do not care for Christ's living in us. On the contrary, it seems that we ourselves are everything. But we should be nothing, and let Him be everything. We all need to realize that we are no longer persons alone, but that we have another One living in us. Christ, our Savior and Redeemer, is living in us right now. We do not merely have His life; we have Him. Therefore, we are no longer alone. Now that He lives in us, we need to learn to live by Him and not by ourselves.

Day after day may go by without our doing anything by Christ. This indicates that we do not practice living by Christ. This is a serious matter. In our daily living we need to practice living by Christ. If we are about to visit the saints or show love, we need to check who is doing it, we or Christ. Before we act, we should wait a while to see whether it is we or Christ who is acting. By doing this we allow the Christ who dwells in us to live for us. This is the practice of the secret.

Paul had been instructed in this secret so that he knew both how to abound and how to be in want. He could do all things in Him. It is sufficient simply to be in Him, for He is all-inclusive and all-sufficient. For example, as we ride in the car, we have complete trust in the car. Christ is more sufficient and more inclusive than any car. Therefore, we should put our full trust in Him. Whatever we do we should do in Him, not in ourselves. We should do everything in Him and by Him. This is the secret Paul learned and the secret we need to learn today. We do not need more teaching, but more practice of this secret. We need to practice doing everything in Him.

NO PREFERENCES

As we practice this secret, we should not have any preference concerning what we do in Him. We, however, may prefer to do certain things in Him, but not other things. We hope that we could keep these things from Him. In this regard, we are like husbands and wives who have secrets from one another. Every husband has kept certain things from his wife, and every wife has kept certain things from her husband. The reason we do this is that we have our own preferences and do not want others to know about them. In the matter of living by Christ we also have preferences. Because of all these preferences, we seldom turn to Him and ask Him what He wants to do in a given situation. But we need to pray, "Lord Jesus, do You want me to do this? If so, show me Your way to do it, Lord." We have Christ living in us, but we may not live by Him or do things in Him. The secret in Philippians 4 is to do all things in Him. The way to experience Christ is to do everything in Him.

For more than fifty years, the Lord has been teaching me to live by Him. I still have not graduated, because l have not been that faithful. Sometimes I was faithful to live by Him for several days. In those days nearly everything I did was in Him. But then I would become unfaithful again. Consider your Christian life. Have you always been faithful in the matter of living by Him and doing all things in Him? Christ does not want us to do anything. He wants to do everything

IN HIM—THE SECRET OF EXPERIENCING CHRIST

for us. In a sense, we have already signed the agreement for Him to do this. This took place on the day we consecrated ourselves to Him. By consecrating ourselves to Him, we offered ourselves to Him. However, after consecrating ourselves, we have not been faithful to live by Him. Rather, we have continued to live by ourselves. Without exception, we all have broken our agreement.

OUR HABIT OF BEING INDEPENDENT

The problem with doing all things in Him is not only a matter of intention, but also a matter of habit. We were born with a fallen nature, and we do not like to do things by others. This is even true of little children. The little ones may not want their mothers to feed them. They prefer to eat by themselves. They want to be free, liberated, and even wild. In this country the young people are anxious to be eighteen years of age, for then they can fly away from the cage of their family. To many, to be free means to be wild. This illustrates the fact that by nature not one of us likes to do things by others. Because we are used to going our own way, it is often troublesome to have Christ living n us.

When I preached the gospel more than forty-five years ago, I told people that we Christians had the most happy life. I asked the unbelievers to join us in this happy life. But later I no longer had the boldness to preach this way, for I learned that as a Christian my life is a life of troubles. I have Someone in me who is always giving me difficulty because He wants to do things differently from the way I would like to do them. Even if I should want to give up being a Christian, He would not let me go. Our problem is that we do not like to do things in Him.

The secret of the Christian life is that another One, Christ, lives in us. Christ is in us, and we must also be in Him. But we do not like to live in Him and with Him, nor do we like doing things by Him. By birth, we have the habit of being independent, and we all have our preferences. But every preference is a suffering, a loss, a failure, a defeat. The reason we do not have a victorious Christian life is that we are not faithful to live by Christ and to do things absolutely in Him.

DOING ALL THINGS BY CHRIST AND IN CHRIST

If you love the Lord, you need to practice doing everything in Him. You need to check whether you are doing things by yourself or by Him. This is the way to gain Christ and to eat Him. To eat properly we should take in one bite at a time. This means that every day, from morning until evening, we should practice living by Christ in all things. We need to do everything with Him. We should be able to say, "From today onward, I shall quit doing things by myself. I do not want to live by myself any longer. From now on I shall live by Him and do everything in Him." If you do this, what a difference there will be in your daily living!

TO LIVE BEING CHRIST

The issue of practicing the secret of doing everything in Christ is that for us to live is Christ. Because we do all things in Christ, for us to live is Christ. The more we do things in Christ, the more we gain of Christ. This is a genuine, absolute enjoyment. However, not many Christians practice the secret of doing all things in Him. Rather, they like to attend meetings and hear messages. But the only way to live is to live by doing everything in Christ. This is the unique way to magnify Christ. In order to magnify Christ, we need to live by Christ and do everything in Christ. We can do all things in Him who empowers us. For example, as long as we are in the car, everything is all right, for the car with the driver can take us where we need to go. As we are riding along in the car, we can enjoy a pleasant time of sight-seeing. Learn to be quiet in Christ, He never makes a mistake. Sometimes, it may seem that He has made a mistake, but actually this is so that you may have a longer ride, enjoy more sight-seeing, and learn more lessons. The Christian life surely is a wonderful life.

As long as we do things in Christ, we shall experience Him, enjoy Him, and accumulate Him. This is the way to become rich in Christ and to have many rich experiences of Christ. If we all are rich in Christ, the meetings will be full of Christ. This is the Lord's recovery. For the recovery, we need to have a rich life in Christ to enrich all the meetings. This is the responsibility not only of the elders, but of all the saints, even the youngest and newest ones. We all need to practice living by Christ and doing all things in Christ. This is the secret that we all need to learn today.

Chapter Eleven

COUNTING GAINS LOSS FOR CHRIST

Of all the Epistles written by Paul only Philippians is clearly and definitely related to the experience of Christ. As we have seen, Philippians comes between Ephesians, a book on the church, and Colossians, a book on the Head. This indicates that in order for us, the members of the Body, to reach the Head, we need the experience of Christ.

LIVING CHRIST AND MAGNIFYING CHRIST

In Philippians 1 Paul says, "Christ shall be magnified in my body" (v. 20), and, "For to me to live is Christ" (v. 21). The statement, "To live is Christ," is simple, but very profound. If we had spoken these words instead of the Apostle Paul, others might accuse us of blasphemy. They might wonder how we could dare say that for us to live is Christ. Paul had the boldness to utter these words because his vision was clear and his experience was rich. Paul had seen clearly that in God's economy for him to live was Christ. He not only saw this, but also lived according to this vision. We also need to have such a clear vision and a rich experience of this matter. We should be able to say, "For us to live is Christ." For us to live is not a good man. For us to live is Christ.

In verse 20 Paul says that Christ would be magnified in his body. Not many Christians know the significance of the word "magnify" in this verse. Some may say that to be magnified means to be expressed, exalted, glorified, or honored. Yes, it does mean these things, but these words do not touch the significance of the word "magnify." For Christ to be magnified in us means that we experience the unlimited Christ. Christ is magnified through His unlimitedness. For example, our love is limited because it is not Christ. The reason there are so many separations and divorces is that human love is limited. Christ is unlimited, but we are limited. If we live by Christ in any matter, that matter will be unlimited. But if we live by ourselves in the same matter, it will be limited. If we love others with our own love, we shall discover that eventually our love will be exhausted. The ones we love will place more and more demands upon us to exhaust our love. The love of a husband is exhausted by his wife, the love of parents is exhausted by their children, and the love of the elders is exhausted by the saints. Although we may be exhausted, Christ is never exhausted. The more love we require, the more love He affords to meet our requirements. Therefore, to live by Christ in the matter of loving others is to magnify Christ by His unlimitedness. The same is true regarding humility and patience. Our humility and patience are limited, but the humility and patience of Christ are unlimited. If we live by Christ in the matters of humility and patience, we magnify Him.

DOGS, EVIL WORKERS, AND THE CONCISION

In the book of Philippians Paul was bold to speak not only in a positive way, but also in a negative way. For example, in 3:2 he said, "Beware of dogs." The Lord Jesus had actually been the first to speak of dogs. In Matthew 7:6 He said, "Do not give that which is holy to the dogs." The "dogs" here refer to the Pharisees, the religious people, the Judaizers. Paul followed the Lord Jesus in telling us to beware of dogs. By the time Paul wrote the book of Philippians, the dogs had become worse than in Matthew 7.

Some may wonder how we can be sure that the dogs in Philippians 3:2 refer to the Judaizers. The proof is in the grammar of this verse. Paul says, "Beware of dogs, beware of evil workers, beware of the concision." In this verse the words "beware of" are used three times. Moreover, there are no conjunctions in this verse, only commas. This indicates that the dogs are the evil workers and that the evil workers are the concision. The word "concision" is a contemptuous word for circumcision. Circumcision is a term of honor, but concision is a term of contempt. Paul purposely referred to

Jewish circumcision in this way. When the Jews who had been circumcised were called the concision, they were being called a people of contempt. Thus, the dogs are the evil workers and the evil workers are the circumcised Jews. Paul was so bold as to call the Judaizers dogs and evil workers. The Jewish religionists, of course, never thought of themselves in this way. Rather, they considered themselves worshippers of God and workers of good, for they tried their best to keep the law. Moreover, to them circumcision was honorable. But in this verse Paul calls them dogs and evil workers and belittles the practice of circumcision by calling it concision.

WORSHIPPING BY THE SPIRIT OF GOD

In verse 3 Paul says, "For we are the circumcision, which worship by the Spirit of God, and boast in Christ Jesus, and trust not in the flesh" (Gk.). "Worship by the Spirit of God" is in contrast to the dogs; "boast in Christ Jesus" is in contrast to evil workers; and "trust not in the flesh" is in contrast to the concision. According to the revelation in these verses, anyone who tries to do something for God without being in the Spirit opposes the genuine worshippers of God in spirit. In the eyes of God, such a person is a dog.

The Lord's word about not giving that which is holy to the dogs indicates that dogs are not holy. The holy things are not for dogs because dogs are not holy. We need to drop the concept that to be holy is simply to be sinless or right and perfect. In the Bible to be holy means to be of God, by God, and with God. Anything that is not of God, by God, and with God is not holy, for in the entire universe God is the only One who is holy. You may be perfect and right, but still not be holy. Only by being a person of God, by God, and with God can we be holy. Thus, to be holy is to be one with God.

For this reason, God the Spirit is called the Holy Spirit. The Spirit of God is God reaching man. When God reaches man, He is the Spirit. No one can contact God except by the Spirit. God cannot reach us except by His Spirit, and we cannot contact Him except by His Spirit. The Spirit by whom we touch God is holy. Therefore, when He reaches us, we become holy. If we do not have something of God, we are not holy at all. But if we are related to God, we become holy.

The first time the word holy is used in the Bible is not in the book of Genesis, but in the book of Exodus. In Genesis it is difficult to find a hint that God became one with man. But in Exodus we see that God begins to be one with man. Therefore, in Exodus, many things are described as being holy: the holy place, the holy mountain, the holy tabernacle, the holy anointing oil. In Exodus many things are described as being holy because in this book God comes to man and man is brought to God.

To be holy is absolutely a matter of the Holy Spirit. Today all the religionists worship God. But it is very doubtful that they worship God by the Spirit of God. Any religionist who does not worship God by the Spirit of God is a dog. Whoever tries to do something for God or to worship God apart from the Spirit is a dog in the eyes of God. This is a serious matter. If we see this vision, it will exercise a strict control over us. We shall be fearful and trembling and we shall say, "I dare not worship God unless I am assured that I am worshipping by the Spirit of God. If I am not in the Spirit, I shall not worship Him." If we see this, there will be a great change in our Christian life. Everything we do for God must be by the Spirit of God. We must have the confidence to say, "We are the circumcision of honor who worship by the Spirit of God."

EXPERIENCING THE SPIRIT BY EMPTYING OURSELVES

Many Christians today do not know the Holy Spirit. They have the terminology, but not the experience. When you are about to worship God or do something for God, you must be reminded not to do these things in yourself. Then you should repudiate yourself and set yourself aside. If there is nothing left after you put yourself aside, then there is nothing of the Holy Spirit in what you are about to do. But if there is something left after you put yourself aside, what remains is the Holy Spirit. This understanding of the Holy Spirit does not come from theology; it comes from experience.

Suppose a bottle is filled with dirt. The more the bottle

is emptied of the dirt, the more air will get into the bottle. The amount of air depends upon the degree of emptiness. Likewise, in order to be filled with the Holy Spirit, we need to empty ourselves. If we empty ourselves, the Holy Spirit will fill us immediately. If we put ourselves aside when we are about to pray, worship, or do something for God, we shall find that the Holy Spirit will be there as the remainder. There is no need for us to speak in tongues in order to have the Holy Spirit. As long as we have a heart for God and the Lord Jesus, the Holy Spirit is with us. But in order to experience the Spirit, we need to empty ourselves.

BEING "DOGS" IN THE EYES OF GOD

Do not worship God in your natural life. One who does this is called a dog by the Apostle Paul. A dog is someone who tries to worship God apart from the Holy Spirit. If we see this, we shall be fearful and pray, "Lord, have mercy upon me. When I pray, I don't want to be a dog, someone who prays in himself."

Some may wonder how anyone can pray to God and still be considered by God as a dog. Have you never accused others in your prayers to God? In the past I have done this many times. I prayed, but as I prayed I accused others. This kind of prayer is certainly not by the Spirit of God. When Saul of Tarsus was persecuting those who called on the name of Jesus, he certainly must have prayed. He might have said, "O God, I am zealous for You and for Your law. Help me to arrest everyone who calls on the name of Jesus." Saul's prayer was like the barking of a dog. Therefore, Paul knew what it meant for the Jewish religionists to be dogs, for he used to be one of those dogs himself. In fact, he was a "top dog" in the Jewish religion. Like Saul of Tarsus, many times our prayers are not by the Spirit of God. This means that we also can be praying dogs. When some hear this, they may say, "No, I am a child of God. Every time I pray, I pray to my heavenly Father." However, the question is by what do you pray, by your natural life or by the Spirit of God. If you pray by your natural life, you are a dog. We should not pray without the Holy Spirit. Neither should we worship God apart from the Spirit of God. We need to be careful regarding our prayer and our worship. We need to pray and worship not by our natural life, but by the Spirit of God.

When the Lord Jesus was on earth, He did not deal mainly with the Gentiles, but with the Jews. Moreover, He mainly dealt with them concerning their worship of God. On one occasion the Lord even called them vipers, something worse than dogs (Matt. 23:33). Do not think that as long as you worship God or pray to God everything is all right. Everything is all right only if you worship and pray by the Spirit of God.

BOASTING IN CHRIST

The second contrast in verses 2 and 3 is the contrast between the evil workers and those who boast in Christ. Whatever we do for God, no matter what it is, is an evil work if it is not Christ. In Matthew 7 the Lord Jesus said that many will come to Him and say that they prophesied in His name, cast out demons in His name, and did many mighty works in His name. However, the Lord will say that they were lawless. This means that what they did was not Christ. Hence, anything we do that is not Christ Himself is evil in the eyes of God, and when we do things that are not Christ we are evil workers. Instead of being evil workers, we must be those who boast in Christ. Our boast must be Christ Himself, not anything of ourselves.

It is not easy for us to boast in Christ. In order to do this, we need to see the vision that anything we do that is not Christ is evil in the eyes of God. God's will is not that we do good things for Him. God's will is that we live out Christ. God only cares for Christ. Therefore, anything we do that is not Christ will not please God. On the contrary, God will consider it evil because it is the doing of our will, not the carrying out of His will. It is actually a form of rebellion. Our works may be good in our eyes, but if they are without Christ, in the eyes of God they are rebellion. If we see this vision, we shall hate not only our hatred, but also our love. When you are about to love someone, you must check whether or not you are loving by Christ. The issue is not one of love or hate; it is whether we act by Christ or by our natural life.

If what we do is something other than Christ, God does not want it. God does not want our love, our humility, or our goodness. God does not want anything of us. He only wants Christ.

EVIL WORKS AND EVIL WORKERS

According to the Gospels, the Pharisees boasted in their good works. But in the eyes of God all their good works were evil. Thus, the Pharisees were evil workers. This is proved by the verses in Philippians 3 where Paul said that he was circumcised the eighth day, that according to law he was a Pharisee, that according to zeal he persecuted the church, and that according to righteousness in the law he was blameless (vv. 5-6). But all these things were evil in the eyes of God because they were not Christ. The Jews boasted that according to the law they were Pharisees, that according to zeal for God they persecuted the churches, and that according to the righteousness of the law they were blameless. In their own eyes they were very good, but in the eyes of God they were evil workers.

The word "evil" here does not denote such things as murder, stealing, or fornication. It refers to something good that is outside of Christ. Even if you do something good, it is an evil work if it is without Christ. We may do many good things, but are these things Christ? If not, we are evil workers. When Paul was Saul of Tarsus, he was such an evil worker. However, at that time he did not realize his real condition. Rather, he thought that he was zealous for God, that he was perfect, righteous, and blameless. He thought this because he was in darkness. But after he received the vision and was enlightened, his eyes were opened to see how foolish he had been. He came to realize that all those good things were actually evil in the eyes of God and that he was an evil worker because he was doing things outside of Christ.

Suppose a certain brother is humble and polite and another brother is tough and rough. We would all prefer the humble brother and regard him as a very good brother. However, the goodness of this brother is outside of Christ. Hence, he is actually an evil worker. Do you have the boldness to say this?

We would all be willing to say that the tough brother is an evil worker, but not the humble brother.

Some may feel that they do not have the ability to discern between Christ and the good points of the natural life. The way to discern is by noticing the difference in weight. Christ is much weightier than anyone's good characteristics. In this way we can make a distinction between these things and Christ. However, we should not weigh others, but ourselves. We need to determine whether our love is weighty or light. If we test our love, we may find that it is as light as a feather. We may also find that our patience and niceness are light, superficial, and easily exhausted. But anything that is of Christ is weighty and long-lasting.

ONLY CHRIST BEING ACCEPTABLE TO GOD

Paul's intention in verses 2 and 3 is to lay the foundation so that in the following verses we may know how to experience Christ. Paul belittled religion to the uttermost, calling the religionists dogs and making light of all natural goodness. If we have Paul's vision, we shall hate our love, our patience, our humility, our niceness, our kindness, and our goodness. I doubt that very many of us have such a practice. Thus, we need the revelation that everything apart from Christ is evil, even the best things. These things are evil because they are a form of rebellion against God's will and against God's economy. God wants us to live out Christ, but we want to live out something else. This is rebellion. We need to see that nothing but Christ Himself is acceptable to God. If we see this, we shall boast in Christ, not in any good works.

HAVING NO TRUST IN THE FLESH

In verse 3 Paul also says that we have no trust in the flesh. Many Christians think that to trust in the flesh means to trust in the fallen human nature. But this is not the meaning of flesh here. In this chapter Paul said that he had reason to trust in the flesh. He goes on to say that he was circumcised on the eighth day, that he was of the race of Israel, that he was of the tribe of Benjamin, that he was a Hebrew of the Hebrews, that according to the law he was a

Pharisee, that according to zeal he persecuted the church, and that according to the righteousness of the law he was blameless. All these things were aspects of Paul's flesh. However, probably you have never regarded such things as the flesh. We think that the flesh includes only evil things, but not good things. Nevertheless, the honorable, lovable, and superior aspects of our natural being are still the flesh. All that Paul did according to the law and according to zeal was flesh and of the flesh. His righteousness according to the law was also flesh. All the seven characteristics listed by Paul in these verses are aspects of the flesh because they all are natural and are neither of Christ nor of the Spirit of God. Anything natural, whether it is good or evil, is the flesh. The Jews trusted in their flesh, trusting in what they were by their natural birth. But we Christians should not trust in anything we have by our natural birth, for anything of our natural birth is part of the flesh.

In order to experience Christ, we need to see that everything we do must be by the Spirit of God, in Christ, and with no trust in the flesh. The flesh denotes all that we are by our natural birth. Both natural foolishness and natural wisdom are of the flesh. Do not think that foolishness is of the flesh and that wisdom is necessarily of the Spirit. As long as it is natural, wisdom is just as fleshly as foolishness. I repeat, in Philippians 3 Paul did not list any negative aspect of the flesh. Everything he mentioned was very good. This indicates that his concept of the flesh was vastly different from ours. To Paul, whatever he was by his natural birth was the flesh. We should not have any trust in our natural being. As long as we have trust in our natural being, we are through with the experience of Christ.

COUNTING THINGS LOSS THAT ONCE WERE GAIN

In order to experience Christ, we must learn to count as loss things that were once a gain to us. We need to count every gain as loss for Christ. There is no comparison between any gain and Christ. If you make such a comparison, you will count everything as loss. The reason we regarded certain things as gain in the past was that we did not know Christ.

But once our eyes were opened to see Christ, we realized how foolish it was to keep those other things. Because Paul had this vision, he could say, "But the things that were gain to me, those I counted loss on account of Christ" (3:7, Gk.).

Only by worshipping by the Spirit of God, by boasting in Christ Jesus, and by not having any trust in our flesh can we be acceptable to God. These three things are basic for the experience of Christ. If we see these things, we shall spontaneously count all things loss for Christ. We shall not treasure them any more. We shall realize that even the best worship of God is the barking of a dog if it is done without the Spirit of God. Even the best things apart from Christ are evil works in the eyes of God. This includes our love, our humility, and our patience. We also need to see that God has no interest in our flesh. If we see this, we shall have no trust in the flesh. If we have the vision regarding these three things, a good foundation will be laid for the experience of Christ.

CHAPTER TWELVE

THE EXCELLENCY OF THE KNOWLEDGE OF CHRIST

In this message we shall consider the excellency of the knowledge of Christ. We all need to have an excellent knowledge regarding Christ. In order to understand what the excellency of the knowledge of Christ is, we need to see some other contrasts in Philippians 3.

In the last message we pointed out the threefold contrast in verses 2 and 3: the contrast between the dogs and the Spirit, between the evil workers and those who boast in Christ, and between the concision and those who have no trust in the flesh. Now we need to see three more contrasts. The Greek word translated "according to" is used three times in verses 5 and 6: according to the law, according to zeal, and according to the righteousness which is in the law. Also in the Greek, the word translated "on account of" used three times in verses 7 and 8: on account of Christ, on account of the excellency of the knowledge of Christ, and on account of whom (Christ). According to the law, Paul was a Pharisee; according to zeal for the law, he persecuted the church; and according to the righteousness which is in the law, he was blameless. Thus, he was a Pharisee, a persecutor, and a blameless one. In these verses we see a contrast between the law and Christ. The law is versus Christ, and Christ is versus the law.

ZEAL AND EXCELLENCY

Also, zeal is in contrast to excellency. An eloquent speaker can stir up our zeal in a few minutes. We also can stir up our zeal by praying for a while. This is especially true of the young people. When they come together, they sometimes say, "We are here to burn one another." After a few minutes of praying, praising, calling, and releasing the spirit, the young people are all burning. This shows that it is quite easy to be zealous. But the excellency of the knowledge of Christ Jesus our Lord does not come so quickly. When Paul wrote the Epistle to the Philippians, he was quite old and had gained much knowledge of Christ. Nevertheless, he still said, "That I may know Him." This indicates that he felt that he was still lacking in the knowledge of Christ. It also indicates that the excellency of the knowledge of Christ does not come easily or quickly. On the contrary, it takes a good deal of time. The entire Bible is a revelation of the wonderful Person of Christ. How excellent and inexhaustible He is! He is far beyond our understanding. Nevertheless, we need to have the excellency of the knowledge of Him.

It is important to have the proper knowledge of things. For example, a jeweler may place a beautiful ring in an attractive jewelry box. If we have the proper knowledge concerning the ring, we shall not treasure the box. Little children, however, may care more for the box than for the ring. They may actually cast aside the ring and fight with one another over the box. The reason they fight over the box is that they do not have the knowledge of the excellency of the ring. Thus, it is crucial to have the excellency of the knowledge concerning certain things.

THE LAW AND CHRIST

The Bible teaches us the law in a negative sense and Christ in a positive sense. If we do not know the law negatively and Christ positively, we do not know the Bible. Religious people care for the law. Anyone who does not have the revelation and the vision of the excellency of Christ will become involved with the law. When people are indifferent toward God, they may not care about morality. But once they begin to care for Him, they will also care for morality and try to live a good life. Immediately, they will become involved with the law. When people are careless, they do not care for God, for morality, or for their behavior. They care only for their pleasure, doing whatever pleases them. Thus, they are lawless. But if such a person turns, repents, and cares for

God, he will also care for morality and behavior. In this way he will come under the law and make up his mind to do good. He will study the Bible to learn how to please God and to benefit others. In other words, he will study the Bible to find out about the law. He will also be eager to receive instruction from those who can teach him to improve his behavior. This kind of religion helps society and the government, for the government certainly desires to have good citizens. Therefore, a religion that teaches people to behave, to be good, and to be peaceful will be welcomed by society.

Many Christians today care more for the law than for Christ. Even learning to pray, to be holy, and to speak in tounges may be matters of the law. The same is true regarding instruction in being a good wife or husband. In the human mentality there is nothing but the law. There is no room, capacity, or ground for Christ. Very few people ever ask me how they can experience Christ in order to be a good husband or wife. It seems that Christians never relate Christ to being a good wife or husband. Most seem to leave Christ far away in the heavens and devote their attention to the law.

All the Judaizers, including Saul of Tarsus, were for the law. They seemed to say, "We Hebrews have the law of God, but the Gentile dogs do not have it." The law was the unique heritage of the Jews, and they gloried and boasted in it. When the Lord Jesus came, He offended the Judaizers because He changed the dispensation of the law to the dispensation of Christ, or of grace. The Judaizers seemed to say, "Are you trying to get rid of our law? We are for the law, and we shall rise up against You. Furthermore, we shall persecute anyone who follows You. According to the righteousness of the law, we are blameless."

THE CASE OF SAUL OF TARSUS

When Paul was Saul of Tarsus, he was such a person, a Pharisee, a persecutor of the church, and one blameless according to the law. According to the law, according to zeal for the Lord, and according to the righteousness of the law, he was perfect, fully qualified to be a "top dog" in Judaism.

But one day a light suddenly shined upon him from heaven, and he fell to the ground. Then he heard a voice saying, "Saul, Saul, why persecutest thou me?" (Acts 9:4). When Saul asked who was speaking to him, the Lord Jesus said, "I am Jesus" (Acts 9:5). Saul was shocked. He thought that Jesus was still in the tomb, but now he heard Him speaking from the heavens. Before that time, Saul saw clearly, but now he was blind. When Paul was Saul of Tarsus, he could say that he was circumcised on the eighth day, that he was of the stock of Israel, that he was of the tribe of Benjamin, that he was a Hebrew of the Hebrews, that according to the law he was a Pharisee, that according to zeal he persecuted the church, and that according to the righteousness of the law he was blameless. But now he was blind. Yet in his blindness he saw Christ. It pleased God the Father to reveal His Son, Jesus Christ, in him. That day on the road to Damascus Paul began to see Christ. However, he did not see Him once for all. Rather, throughout the years, he saw Him again and again.

Because Paul had come to know Christ, he obtained the excellency of the knowledge of Christ. On account of this excellency, he counted all things loss. Paul counted all things loss first on account of Christ, then on account of the excellency of the knowledge of Christ.

ON ACCOUNT OF CHRIST

Tn Philippians 3 Paul shows that Christ is versus the law. In this chapter we see two contrasting phrases: "according to the law" and "on account of Christ." Are you a person according to something, or a person on account of something? We should not be people according to anything, but people on account of Christ, on account of a wonderful Person. We are not here according to religion or even according to the Lord's recovery. We are here on account of the Person of Christ. Moreover, we are not even according to Christ, but on account of Christ. To be according to something is to imitate it or to follow it outwardly. But to be on account of something means that thing gets into us. We are on account of Christ because Christ has come into us. In Philippians 3 Paul seemed to be saying, "On account of Christ, I count all things loss. According to the law, I was a Pharisee; according to zeal, I persecuted the church; and according to the righteousness of the law, I was blameless. I worked and behaved according to the law. But I am no longer a man according to the law. Now I am a man on account of Christ. Christ has changed my life and revolutionized my whole being. He has come into me to be my life, my nature, and even my disposition. I am now on account of Him. On account of Him, I have counted as loss every religious and natural gain." Paul also said that he counted all things loss on account of the excellency of the knowledge of Christ Jesus the Lord. How excellent Christ is! However, many traditional Christians oppose the excellency of Christ.

A wonderful Person, Christ, has visited me and has come into me. Now He is taking possession of me and making His home in me. Many times He makes me happy, but sometimes He causes me to be unhappy. A few times I have even begged Him to leave, but He always refuses. Once He has come in, He will remain forever. Neither anything religious nor anything natural can be compared with Him.

THE FATHER REVEALING THE SON TO US

In Matthew 11:27 the Lord Jesus said that no one knows the Son except the Father. When I first read this verse, I was disappointed, wondering how I could ever know Christ. But in Matthew 16 we see that it is possible for us to know Christ through the Father's revelation of Him. The revelation concerning the Son was given to Peter by the Father. When Peter confessed that Jesus was the Christ, the Son of the living God, the Lord Jesus said, "Flesh and blood did not reveal this to you, but My Father Who is in the heavens" (Matt. 16:17). Only the Father knows the Son. Yet, the Father wants to reveal Him to us.

CHRIST REVEALED IN VARIOUS BOOKS
OF THE NEW TESTAMENT

The Gospel of John reveals Christ to us. In John 1:1 we see that Christ is God Himself. Surely the law cannot compare to God. How foolish it is to keep the law and neglect God!

The law may produce religious "dogs," but God begets sons. According to the book of Revelation, the holy sons of God are in the holy city, but the dogs are outside (Rev. 22:15).

According to the first chapter of John, Christ was not only God, but the very means, the channel, through which everything came into being. This means that He was the Creator. Furthermore, John 1:4 says, "In Him was life." One day this wonderful One became flesh, and, having become flesh, He became the tabernacle of God (John 1:14). As the tabernacle, He had the glory of the Father, and with Him were grace and reality (John 1:14). Out of His fullness, we have received grace upon grace. This One declared God whom no one had ever seen.

Acts 2 reveals that the very Jesus who was crucified on the cross has been exalted by God to be the Lord and the Christ. Today Jesus is Lord and Christ, the anointed and appointed One of God. In Romans 1:4 we are told that Christ was designated in the power of resurrection by the Spirit of holiness to be the Son of God. This One is over all, God blessed forever (Rom. 9:5). One day this Person became the life-giving Spirit (1 Cor. 15:45). What a wonderful Person He is!

In Colossians we see more of the excellency of the knowledge of Christ. Colossians 1:15 says that He is the image of the invisible God. Colossians 1:15-17 go on to say that Christ is also the Creator as well as the Firstborn of creation, the first item of all the creatures. Moreover, not only were all things created in Him, but they also subsist in Him, for He holds all things together. I once read an article that said that some power at the center of the universe is holding the universe together. If this power were removed, the entire universe would collapse. This holding power in which all things subsist is Christ. He is the hub of the universe; all the spokes are joined to Him. Colossians 1 also reveals that Christ is the Firstborn from the dead in resurrection and that He is the Head of the church (v. 18). Verse 19 goes on to say that God the Father is pleased that all His fullness would dwell in Christ.

Colossians 2:2 says that Christ, the wonderful One, is the

mystery of God; 2:9, that the fullness of the Godhead dwells in Christ bodily; and 3:4, that He is even our life. How marvelous and inexhaustible He is!

Hebrews 1:2 and 3 say that Christ is the heir of all things, the effulgence of God's glory, and the express image of God's substance. Through Him all things were made, and He upholds all things by the word of His power. Elsewhere in Hebrews we see that He is the High Priest in the heavens (4:14), a Priest not according to the law of letters, but according to the power of an indestructible life (7:16). He is also the Mediator of a better covenant (Heb. 8:6).

Finally, the book of Revelation shows us that this wonderful One is the redeeming Lamb with seven eyes, which are the seven Spirits of God (Rev. 5:6). There are a great many other aspects of Christ revealed in the New Testament. But these are sufficient to show us something of the excellency of the knowledge of Christ.

COUNTING ALL THINGS LOSS

Let us return to the illustration of the gold ring in the attractive box. If children have the excellency of the knowledge of the ring, they will not fight over the box. Instead, they will seek to gain possession of the ring. Before his experience on the road to Damascus, Paul did not have the excellency of the knowledge of Christ. He treasured the law and was zealous and righteous according to the law. But one day his eyes were opened to see the excellency of the knowledge of the wonderful One. On account of this excellency, he counted as loss all things, whether they were related to religious gain or natural gain. Paul said that he counted all things loss for the excellency of the knowledge of Christ Jesus the Lord. Christ refers to God's anointed and appointed One, the Messiah, who accomplishes everything God has purposed. Jesus is the name of the Nazarene who lived in Palestine. Today Jesus Christ is our Lord. This means that He has something to do with us. On account of the excellency of the knowledge of this wonderful One, we count all things loss. Furthermore, we even suffer the loss of all things. I would like to cast everything aside on account of this Person.

Compared to Him, all other things are dung, dog food. When Paul was one of the "dogs" in Judaism, he needed dog food. But when he became a son of the living God, he had no further need for it. In its place, he had better food, the wonderful Person of Christ Himself. We are no longer dogs feeding on refuse; we are sons of God feeding on Christ Jesus our Lord.

May we all have more of the excellency of the knowledge of Christ. If we do, we shall drop everything religious and everything natural on account of Him and on account of the excellency of the knowledge of Him. When we worship by the Spirit of God, boast in Christ Jesus, have no trust in the flesh, and have the excellency of the knowledge of Christ Jesus the Lord, we have the proper basis for the experience of Christ.

Chapter Thirteen

TO GAIN CHRIST AND BE FOUND IN HIM

In the previous message we covered the three occurrences of the phrase "on account of" in Philippians 3:7 and 8. On account of Christ, Paul counted as loss the things which were gain to him; on account of the excellency of the knowledge of Christ Jesus the Lord, he counted all things loss; and on account of Christ Jesus the Lord, he suffered the loss of all things and counted them dung. This is in contrast to the three occurrences of "according to" in verses 5 and 6: according to the law, according to zeal, and according to the righteousness that is in the law.

A CAUSE PRODUCING AN EFFECT

These three uses of "on account of" indicate a cause that produces an effect. On account of Christ, Paul counted as loss all religious gain and all gain from his natural birth. On account of the excellency of the knowledge of Christ, he counted everything loss. Moreover, on account of Christ Jesus the Lord, he suffered the loss of all things. On account of Christ, the all-inclusive Person, he forsook everything and gave up everything.

We need to be impressed with the all-inclusiveness of Christ. The Gospel of John reveals that Christ is God, that He is the Creator, that in Him is life, and that this life is the light of men (John 1:1-4). One day, He, the Word, became flesh, full of grace and truth (v. 14). According to Colossians, Christ is the image of the invisible God, the Firstborn of every creature, and the One in whom all things were made and in whom they consist (Col. 1:15-17). Christ holds together in Himself the entire universe. Hebrews 1:3 says that He upholds all things by the word of His power. For example, the planet earth is neither too close to the sun nor too far from it. If the earth were too close, it would be burned, and if it were too far, it would be frozen. The Lord Jesus Christ is the One responsible for keeping the earth in its proper position in relation to the sun. The very Christ who does this is also our life. If He can regulate the earth and the sun, then He can certainly regulate us, and He can surely regulate our relationship with our husband or wife. The Christ who upholds the universe and in whom all things consist upholds the relationship between a husband and his wife. The reason so many marriages end in divorce is that in those marriages there are two spokes without a hub. Hallelujah, we have the all-inclusive Christ as our hub!

Colossians 1:18 goes on to say that Christ is the Firstborn from the dead. Hence, He is not only the Firstborn in creation, but also the Firstborn in resurrection. Both in the old creation and in the new creation, He is the Firstborn. Therefore, He is the Head of the church. Colossians also reveals that it pleased the Father that all His fullness would be embodied in Christ (1:19).

Many who talk about Christ speak of Him in a light, superficial way. Christ is unlimited. We need to have the excellency of the knowledge of this unlimited Christ, who is our Lord. On account of this Person, Christ Jesus the Lord, the Apostle Paul suffered the loss of all things. This was the cause. The effect issuing from this cause was that Paul gained Christ. On account of Christ, he suffered the loss of all things in order that he might gain Christ.

GAINING CHRIST

What does it mean to gain Christ? According to the Greek, the noun form of the word "gain" is in verse 7, and the verbal form is in verse 8. Therefore, Darby translates verse 8 this way: "That I may have Christ as gain." To gain Christ means to have Christ as gain. Paul seemed to be saying, "In the past, so many religious things were gain to me. Also, the things I had according to my birthright were gain to me. But on account of the excellency of the knowledge of Christ, I have forsaken all these gains so that I may obtain Christ as my gain." This gain comes by revelation. We need to be unveiled to see Christ in the various books of the New Testament, in John, Romans, Colossians, Hebrews, and Revelation. We need to see that Christ is over all, God blessed forever (Rom. 9:5). But to see Christ is not merely for the sake of seeing Him; to see Him is for the sake of gaining Him. After seeing Christ, we need to gain Him.

Take shopping in a supermarket as an example. You may see many things in the store, but seeing them does not mean that they belong to you. In order for the items to belong to you, you need to pay the price for them. I have no doubt that we have all seen something of Christ. But now we must pay the price in order to gain what we have seen. This is the reason that verse 8 speaks of the excellency of the knowledge of Christ and that at the end of this verse Paul says, "In order that I may gain Christ" (Gk.). Seeing the things concerning Christ causes us to gain Christ. However, simply to see may not cost us anything, for seeing something does not necessarily mean that we have paid the price to gain it. Nevertheless, seeing causes us to gain. In order to gain, we must pay the price. Paul not only saw the excellency of Christ, but paid the price to gain Him. On account of Christ, he suffered the loss of all things. This indicates that he paid the price. In Philippians 3 Paul seemed to be saying, "I have not only counted all things loss, but suffered the loss of all things in order that I may gain Christ." My burden in this message is to help you to see Christ and especially to gain Christ. To see Christ is one thing, and to gain Christ is another.

In gaining Christ we should not go window shopping. When people go window shopping, they look at certain items, but they do not buy them. Some brothers and sisters in the church life come to the meetings in the way of window shopping. They enjoy listening to the messages, but they do not pay the price to gain Christ. To pay the price is to suffer the loss of all things. First, Paul counted as loss all religious gain and all gain by natural birth. Then he counted all things loss and suffered the loss of all things. He did this in order to gain the Christ he had seen. A number of times I have spent a large amount of money to buy a particular item. After purchasing that item and bringing it home, I began to regret the price I had paid for it. However, when I considered the item and realized the excellency of it, I did not care about the price I had paid. This is why Paul said that after suffering the loss of all things, he counted them dung. What he paid to gain Christ was nothing but dung, dog food, trash, rubbish, refuse. He did not regret the price he had paid.

Having spent a great deal of time on Philippians 3, I believe that I have entered into Paul's spirit in this chapter. Paul suffered the loss of all things and counted them dung in order that he might gain Christ. Even this is simply a gaining by revelation. If a sister buys food at the market, brings it home, and puts it into the refrigerator, she does not yet have the food in reality. No, the food must be cooked and eaten by her and her family. For example, it is not a simple process for me to take some chicken into me, for my wife must go to the market, buy the chicken, bring it home, and cook it. Then I need to eat it. The point of this illustration is that we may see something, pay the price for it, and gain it, but still not actually have that thing because we have not yet taken it into us. This is the reason that after speaking about gaining Christ, Paul said, "And be found in him" (v. 9). To see Christ is one thing, to gain Christ is another thing, and to be found in Christ is still another thing.

Before going on to the matter of being found in Christ, I would like to emphasize more the need to gain Him. I am concerned that many of us have seen something of Christ, but have not gained very much of Him. Here in Philippians 3, to gain Christ is to get Christ through revelation. In Galatians 1 Paul said that it pleased God to reveal His Son in him. Although God is pleased to reveal Christ in us, we still need to receive Christ by paying the price. This was the reason Paul had the boldness to say that he suffered the loss of all things. For Saul of Tarsus to receive God's revelation concerning Christ was a very significant thing. Paul was a leader in the Jewish religion, he had made a name for himself, and he was very zealous. There was a great deal of gain for him in that religion. Suddenly, God intervened to trouble him and seemed to say, "Saul, what are you doing? I know that you have reached the top in religion, that you are zealous, and that you have earned a name for yourself. But I have come to show you something better. Saul, what you have is just dog food." It was not easy for Saul to give up his position in Judaism and take another way.

I am concerned for those who merely come to the meetings, listen to messages, and read the printed materials. They may see something of Christ, but they may not pay the price to gain what they have seen. Paul received the excellency of the knowledge of Christ, and he suffered the loss of all things, thereby paying the price to gain what he saw. He paid and he gained. But this is not all; he also desired to be found in Christ.

BEING FOUND IN CHRIST

To be found in Christ actually is to live in Christ. Angels are constantly watching us, and so are the people around us. Both observed Paul to see the way he lived. He used to be in Judaism, but now he was in Christ. He used to be zealous for the law, but now he was burning for Christ. Paul realized that he was under the observation both of angels and Judaizers. Hence, he said that he wanted to gain Christ and be found in Him. He wanted the angels, the Judaizers, and everyone around him to see that he was one who lived in Christ, that he not only gained Christ, but was to be found in Christ. Paul saw Christ and paid the price for Christ in order that he might gain Christ. Moreover, he lived by Christ and in Christ. He was a man in Christ (2 Cor. 12:2). Day by day and hour by hour, Paul lived in Christ. Thus, he had the boldness to say, "To me to live is Christ" (Phil. 1:21). At any time, Paul could be found in Christ. If we could ask Timothy or Titus, they could tell us that they always found Paul in Christ. Suppose after giving this message I go home and smoke a pipe. If you find me doing that, you will find me, not in Christ, but in smoking. The same will be true if I lose my temper with my wife, gossip about the saints, or criticize the meetings. In such a case I will be found not in Christ, but in the act of losing my temper, gossiping, or criticizing.

This matter of being found in Christ is not mere theology; it is a matter of the practical experience of Christ. First, we need to see the revelation of the excellency of the knowledge of Christ. Second, we need to pay the price that we may gain Christ. Third, we need to live in Christ, remain in Christ, lodge in Christ, speak in Christ, act in Christ, and move in Christ. We need to have our being in Christ. Then whenever an angel or a saint finds us, we shall be found in Christ. Our being found in Christ will surprise the demons and terrify the Devil. Oh, that we may gain Christ and be found in Him! Being found in Christ is not a once for all matter. On the contrary, it is a daily matter, an hourly matter. If men do not know where we are, at least the angels know. Others may not be able to see us, but the angels know whether or not we are in Christ. Day by day and hour by hour, we need to be found in Christ by the angelic eyes that are watching us. Where do we live, work, and have our being? We need to be found in Christ by the angels, by our husband or wife, and by the brothers and sisters in the church. This is a serious matter.

Today it is not a matter of law, regulation, or a way of living. Rather, it is absolutely a matter of Christ. Have you seen Christ? Have you gained Christ? Are you found in Christ by both men and angels? In our daily living we need to be able to declare that for us to live is Christ.

NOT HAVING OUR OWN RIGHTEOUSNESS, BUT GOD'S RIGHTEOUSNESS

In verse 9 Paul also says, "Not having mine own righteousness." This phrase modifies the word "found." We need to be found in Christ in a condition of not having our own righteousness, which is of the law, but having the righteousness that is by the faith of Christ, the righteousness which is out from God by faith. Paul did not have his own righteousness; he had God's righteousness. Righteousness refers to proper and upright living, to a life that is right. Paul was found by the angels and by all who were around him in a condition of not having his upright living out from himself, but out from God. This means that God was lived out of Paul. As he was in Christ, having his being in Christ, and moving, walking, and doing everything in Christ, Paul lived out God. Thus, God was expressed in his right living. His living was not his behavior; it was God Himself.

Doctrinally it is difficult to tell whether a brother's righteousness is his own or is the expression of God. But it is quite easy to tell by discerning the scent of his righteousness. By our sense of smell, not by our sense of sight, we can discern a pleasant scent from a disagreeable one. For example, a certain kind of love may give off an odor that makes us sick. This kind of love is not only natural, human love, but fleshly love. Although it is love, it has a very foul odor. In other cases we can smell a love that is heavenly, fresh, pure, sweet, and divine. This kind of love is the expression of the love of God; it is the loving God manifested through His children. This is the righteousness which is out from God and based upon faith.

THE FAITH OF CHRIST

The righteousness that is based upon faith is conditioned by faith. It does not come by our efforts, endeavors, or struggles. It comes simply by the faith of Christ. Hence, there is no need for us to strive, struggle, or endeavor. We simply need to gain Christ, live in Him, and even rest in Him. Christ is my faith. I have been crucified with Christ, Christ lives in me, and the life which I live I live by the faith of Christ (Gal. 2:20). My living today is conditioned by Christ's faith. It is based upon the faith of Christ, not upon a faith that I myself can produce. Thus, Christ is not only my life; He is also my faith. By faith, I repudiate myself and take Christ as my life. Because I have no trust in my flesh, I set it aside, take Christ by faith, and live by Him. Spontaneously, God is lived out of me, manifested through me, and expressed from within me. Such a living is a proper and upright living.

This type of upright living is not according to the law, but on account of God, for it is God Himself expressed through us. Because most of today's Christians do not see this, they are living in another realm, in another sphere. But we are in the sphere of Christ, living out God from within us. This is not a matter of behaving or struggling, but of resting. We simply need to rest in Him, resting in our Lord who is our life and our faith. In this way we live out God as our upright living. This is the righteousness out from God based upon faith. May we all be found in Christ in this condition! Day by day, angels and all who are around us need to find us in such a condition. We should be able to say, "Angels, look at the Christians in the Lord's recovery. They are in a condition of having God lived out of them. They don't care for behavior or conduct. They care only for taking Christ as their life. They always take Christ as life and rest in Him. Whenever you see them, you find them in Christ in a condition of having God lived out of them." This is the proper church life with a living testimony. This is what the Lord desires today. Oh, that we may gain Christ and be found in Him, not having our own righteousness which is out from the law, but having the righteousness which is by the faith of Christ, the righteousness which is out from God based upon faith! May we gain Christ and be found in Him in such a condition!

CHAPTER FOURTEEN

TO KNOW HIM

In Philippians 3:8 Paul speaks of the excellency of the knowledge of Christ. In verse 10 he says, "To know Him" (Gk.). According to grammar, the phrase "to know Him" is an infinitive and needs to follow another word, but there is a question as to what word it follows. There are two possibilities: the first, that it follows "to be found in Him"; and the second, that it follows the word "faith." Scholars disagree with one another concerning this matter. According to our experience, I would say strongly that I do not agree with the first view, but that I am absolutely for the second, that "to know Him" follows the modifying phrase ending with the word "faith."

PAUL'S TURN FROM THE LAW TO CHRIST

If this view is correct, then here the Apostle Paul seemed to be saying, "When I was Saul of Tarsus, everyone always found me in the law. Day and night, I was in the law, and I was found by others in the law. Even the angels knew how much I was in the law. I was simply a man in the law. My heart, mind, emotion, and motive, thought, intention, and activity were altogether in the law. Because I was so much for the law, my whole being was in the law. But that day on the road to Damascus I was turned from the law to Christ. It pleased God to reveal His Son, Christ, in me, and I was willing to pay the price by selling my status in Judaism. I was of the stock of Israel and of the tribe of Benjamin, that lovable and honorable tribe. I was a Hebrew of the Hebrews and a Pharisee. I was zealous and blameless. I certainly had a superior status. But the heavenly vision turned me from the law to Jesus, the very One I had been persecuting. The heavenly vision was so strong and subduing that it defeated and conquered me." Thus, Saul of Tarsus surrendered to the Lord and was willing to sell his status in Judaism. From that time onward, he began to count as loss all religious and natural gain, selling them for the excellency of the knowledge of Christ, so that he might gain Christ and be found in Him. From the time of his vision on the way to Damascus, his whole life was changed. Neither the angels nor those around him could find him in the law any longer. No matter who found him, when he was found, he was found in Christ. No matter what he was doing, he was in Christ. While he was teaching, he was in Christ. While he was ministering, he was in Christ. While he was moving and acting, he was in Christ. Day and night, he was a man in Christ. He was always found in Christ in a condition of having no righteousness of his own out from the law. This means that he did not do good according to the law by his natural life. He was found in Christ in a condition of having a righteousness that was the expression of God. Hence, he did not have the righteousness that was out from the law, but the righteousness that was out from God. Therefore, he did not act, behave, perform, strive, or struggle; on the contrary, he simply believed, believing not by his own faith, but by Jesus Christ as his faith.

TAKING CHRIST AS FAITH

Paul took Christ, not only as his life, but also as his faith. In Galatians 2:20 he said that he was crucified with Christ, that he lived no longer, and that Christ lived in him; he continued on to say that the life he lived was by the faith of the Son of God who loved him and died for him. This verse reveals that Christ lived in Paul and that Paul lived not only by Christ's life, but also by Christ's faith. In himself, Paul had no faith. Even the faith by which Paul lived was the faith of Christ. This means that Paul was found in Christ in the condition that he lived by Christ as his faith and thereby lived out God as his righteousness. His righteousness was not behavior or conduct; it was God Himself lived out of him as his righteousness by faith. It was in this condition that Paul sought to know Christ.

KNOWING CHRIST THROUGH EXPERIENCE

Since Paul already had the excellency of the knowledge of Christ, why was he still seeking to know Him? The excellency of the knowledge of Christ comes by revelation. But the knowing of Him spoken of in verse 10 comes not by revelation, but by experience. According to my experience, the word "know" here is equal to "experience." To know Him means to experience Him, to enjoy Him, to participate in Him, and to partake of Him. Take eating as an example. First you select certain groceries, you pay for them, and then you cook them. By eating what you have cooked, you come to know the food you have bought. In like manner we also need to pay the price to gain Christ and to be found in Him, not having the righteousness which is out from ourselves, but the righteousness that is God Himself lived out of our being in faith. In such a condition we are to know Christ through experiencing Him a little at a time. It is not sufficient to listen to messages and to see Christ by revelation.

THE GOSPELS AS A RECORD OF LIFE

As one who was raised in Christianity, I heard the stories of Jesus from the time I was a little child. Both at home and in Sunday school, I was taught the stories in the Gospels concerning Christ. For a long time, the Gospels were nothing more than stories to me. After I was saved, I no longer considered them as mere stories, but viewed them as containing lessons for me to learn. Later, I changed my concept again, this time from lessons to teachings. Along with learning the teachings, I was also told to take Christ as my example, for, according to the lessons and teachings, Christ was to be our example and pattern. Many Christians today consider the four Gospels mainly as stories, lessons, teachings, and examples. However, twice the Lord Jesus said that He was life (John 11:25; 14:6). Thus, whatever is recorded in the Gospels is life, not merely stories, lessons, teachings, or examples.

In the Gospels we see that life is a Person, not a thing,

condition, or situation. Paul said in Philippians 3 that he wanted to gain Christ and be found in Him. The One whom he wanted to gain and in whom he wanted to be found was Christ Jesus as his life. This means that Paul wanted to be found in life, in the Person who was his life. Furthermore, as we have pointed out, Paul wanted to be found in Him in a condition of not having the righteousness that was out from himself according to the law, but of having the righteousness that was God lived out of him in faith. Therefore, Paul could say, "I want to be found in the One who is my life in such a condition that I have nothing out from myself, but only the living God lived out of me as my righteousness by the faith of Christ." The condition in which Paul desired to be found was a condition according to faith, not according to work. Paul could be in such a condition only by believing, not by doing or struggling. He wanted to be in this condition that he might know Christ, that is, that he might experience, enjoy, participate in, and partake of all that Christ was to him.

At this point, we need to consider the book of 2 Corinthians, which may be considered Paul's autobiography. Brother Nee once pointed out that the book of Deuteronomy is the autobiography of Moses. If you want to know the kind of person Moses was, you need to study this book. Likewise, if you want to know the kind of person the Apostle Paul was, you need to read 2 Corinthians. In this book Paul wrote of his personal life.

LIVING IN THE PERSON OF CHRIST

Second Corinthians 2:10 says, "To whom ye forgive anything, I forgive also: for if I forgave anything, to whom I forgave it, for your sakes forgave I it in the person of Christ." What does it mean to say that Paul forgave in the person of Christ? I spent a long time studying this verse before I came to realize Paul's meaning. My understanding of this is best expressed through an illustration. Once I was invited to a brother's home for dinner. At a certain point I asked the brother a question, and then I turned the question to his wife. Before she answered me, she first looked at her husband, and he looked at her. Learning from the look in her husband's eyes what to say, she proceeded to answer me in the person of her husband. Many husbands and wives relate to one another in this way. If a wife does not know how to behave in the person of her husband, she is independent. A wife should always speak in the person of her husband. Any wife who speaks according to the person of her husband is a very good wife, for she lives not by herself, but by her husband. Although she has her own personality, she does not live by her personality, but by the person of her husband. How wonderful this is!

All the young people need to learn how to live in the person of Christ. The way to experience Christ is to live in the person of Christ. We need to do everything in the person of Christ. For example, if you can watch television in the person of Christ, go ahead and do it. But if you honestly cannot watch it in the person of Christ, you should not do it. If you look at the Lord as you are watching television, He may tell you to shut if off. Furthermore, a married brother must learn to speak to his wife in the person of Christ. If he lives in the person of Christ with his wife, he will not argue with her. If he checks with the Lord as he is about to exchange words with her, the Lord will tell him to stop. What a wonderful life we would have if we lived in the person of Christ!

Paul was one who lived in the person of Christ. According to 2 Corinthians 2:10, he forgave in the person of Christ. Paul did not do anything according to his choice, taste, or preference. Instead, he did everything according to the taste of Christ. The best wife is one who lives by taking her husband as her person. The husbands also need to live in the person of their wives, but with discernment. This is according to God's economy. According to God's household arrangement, the headship is not with the wife, but with the husband. Nevertheless, both the wife and the husband need to live in the person of the other party. Then their married life will be sweet and pleasant. What a wonderful experience it is to live in the person of Christ!

According to the Greek text, the Greek word rendered "person" in 2 Corinthians 2:10 is the same word as the word translated "face" in 2 Corinthians 4:6, the verse which says that the glory of God is in the face of Jesus Christ. This indicates that when Paul lived in the person of Christ, he lived in the face of Christ. He was a man in Christ, who was found in Christ in a condition based upon faith and conditioned by faith. In order to know Christ in his daily experience, Paul did everything in the person of Christ. Christ and he were not two, but one. Therefore, in Philippians 1:21 he could say, "For to me to live is Christ." He lived in the person of Christ and was one with Christ. Two persons, Paul and Christ, lived as one. We need such a life as this.

THE MEEKNESS AND CONSIDERATENESS OF CHRIST

Second Corinthians 10:1 says, "Now I Paul myself beseech you by the meekness and considerateness of Christ" (Gk.). This verse does not mean, however, that Paul was imitating Christ. No, because he lived by Christ, Christ's meekness became his. Hence, he could beseech the Corinthians through the meekness of the Christ by whom he lived. Paul was meek, not in himself, but in Christ. Whatever he expressed as meekness was Christ's meekness, not his own.

Furthermore, Paul also besought the Corinthians by the considerateness of Christ. Other versions render the Greek word here as "lenience." This means that Paul was not legal, but was flexible and lenient. Like his meekness, his lenience was not of himself; it was of Christ. Paul experienced Christ as the One who was kind, gentle, and flexible. Because he lived by Christ, Christ's lenience was his. Because Paul lived by Christ, he had the virtues of Christ, including the virtues of meekness and considerateness. In his ministry, writing, and speaking, Paul was in Christ. Everything he did was done by the virtues of Christ. In everything we do we need to be found in Christ. Oh, that I may gain Christ and be found in Him in a condition that is based upon faith! I do not want to do anything by my struggling or endeavoring. Rather, I want to do everything by living in Christ that His virtues may be spontaneously expressed in my living.

THE TRUTH OF CHRIST

In 2 Corinthians 11:10 Paul says, "The truth of Christ is

in me." The truth of Christ was in Paul because Christ Himself was in him. Christ is the truth. This is a further proof that Paul lived by Christ. Otherwise, he could not have had the truth of Christ.

THE GRACE OF CHRIST BEING SUFFICIENT

In chapter twelve Paul prayed three times that the thorn in his flesh would depart from him. Verse 9 says, "And he said unto me, My grace is sufficient for thee: for my strength is made perfect in weakness. Most gladly therefore will I rather glory in my infirmities, that the power of Christ may rest upon me." The power of Christ overshadowed Paul, tabernacling over him. This also is the experience of Christ. Paul did not do anything on his own, nor did he insist upon his preference. He simply looked to Christ, trusted in Christ, lived by Christ, and learned to enjoy Christ's overshadowing. To him, Christ was a tabernacle overshadowing him, no matter what difficulties he was experiencing. Under this overshadowing, Paul enjoyed God's sufficient grace. Therefore, little by little and step by step, he came to know Christ, not only by revelation, but through his personal experience. He could testify and boast that the grace of Christ was sufficient. He knew that when he was weak, he was strong, because in his weakness the power of Christ was made perfect. This is the living out of Christ. What an experience of Christ the Apostle Paul had!

A MAN IN CHRIST

In 2 Corinthians 12:2 Paul said, "I knew a man in Christ." Paul referred to himself as a man in Christ. What a marvelous designation! I hope that we all shall be able to refer to ourselves in this way. I hope after some years, you will be able to look back and say, referring to yourself, "Seven years ago, I knew a man in Christ."

THE REVELATION OF A WONDERFUL PERSON

Let us consider the four Gospels once again. I have already pointed out that it is possible to take the Gospels as stories, lessons, teachings, and examples. But the primary thing about the Gospels is that they present a Person who is life. I am still coming to know the Lord as He is revealed in the Gospels. How sweet is the record in the Gospels of the One who is my life! To me, the Gospels are no longer books of stories, lessons, teachings, or examples. They are the revelation of a wonderful Person. This Person is the very God who created all things. In Him was life. One day, He became flesh, full of glory, grace, and reality; and of His fullness we have received grace upon grace. This One lived on earth until He was betrayed, arrested, condemned, and crucified. Then He was buried. On the third day He was resurrected to become the heavenly *pneuma* breathed into His disciples (John 20:22). From that time onward, He was in the disciples. However, He is also the One who has ascended into the heavens.

When the Lord Jesus was on earth, He always lived a life under the death of the cross that dealt with His natural life. Even before He was put on the cross, He lived under the cross by denying His natural life so that His divine life could be released in the power of resurrection. Realizing this has changed my view of the Gospels. It has helped me to know Christ not simply by revelation, but by daily experience. Day by day, I experience a little more of Him. Now whenever I open any page of the Gospels, I see this wonderful Person and experience Him. This means that I taste Him, enjoy Him, and partake of Him. In eternity I shall still be enjoying Him and partaking of Him. The very Jesus Christ revealed in the four Gospels is our life; we need to know Him in this way.

Firstly, God has been pleased to reveal Christ into us. Secondly, we must all be willing to pay the price to receive this revelation that we may gain Christ. Thirdly, we need not only to gain Him, but also to live in Him and be found in Him by angels and by all those around us. In Him we live in a situation that is regulated and conditioned by faith. Little by little, we need to know Him experientially. This is the way to experience Christ and to know Christ.

After we receive the divine revelation, we have the experience of Christ as life. In this way we know Christ, not in theory, but in our daily experience, and His virtues are lived out in our humanity. If we need meekness, He is our meekness. If we need truth, He is our truth. He even becomes our very person. Thus, we live in Him by taking Him as our person and by doing everything in the person of Christ. This is the proper and normal Christian life. The normal Christian life is not good behavior or improved conduct. The one who lives a normal Christian life lives in the person of Christ to live out God as his righteousness without struggling or striving, but with rest and enjoyment. What a life of enjoyment this is! Such a life is our daily salvation.

CHAPTER FIFTEEN

TO KNOW THE POWER OF HIS RESURRECTION

In this message we shall continue to dwell on Philippians 3:10, one of the great verses in the New Testament. This verse speaks of four things: knowing Christ, knowing the power of His resurrection, knowing the fellowship of His sufferings, and being conformed to His death. Thus, four things are included in this verse: Christ, the power of His resurrection, the fellowship of His sufferings, and the conformity to His death.

Not many Christians have a proper understanding of the power of Christ's resurrection or the fellowship of His sufferings. Many do not even know much about His sufferings, knowing only that He suffered during His crucifixion. But this verse speaks of sufferings, not suffering. Knowing Christ, knowing the power of His resurrection, knowing the fellowship of His sufferings, and being conformed to His death are all related to our experience of Christ. If we would experience Christ, we must know Him. Knowing Him depends on how much we know the power of His resurrection and the fellowship of His sufferings. Hence, knowing the power of His resurrection and the fellowship of His sufferings is vital in our knowing Him.

The New Testament clearly reveals that resurrection, especially the resurrection of Christ, is related to death. Without death, there is no need of resurrection and no opportunity for resurrection to be manifested. In order to know the power of resurrection, we must enter into a death situation and remain there. Since it is necessary to be in death in order to know the power of resurrection, we must understand what it means to be in death.

A CRUCIFIED LIFE

For this understanding, we need to consider the record of the life of the Lord Jesus as found in the four Gospels. The Gospels are not merely an account of stories, lessons, teachings, or examples, but a record of a Person who is our life. According to the record of the Gospels, His life is a crucified life. Not only was Christ crucified when He was put on the cross; before He was put on the cross, He lived under the cross. In other words, He continually lived a crucified life. This means that He always put Himself under the death of the cross that He might be terminated. Christ was constantly being crucified; nevertheless, He lived.

Galatians 2:20 says, "I am crucified with Christ: nevertheless I live; yet not I, but Christ liveth in me." In this verse there are three significant words: nevertheless...yet...but. Hence, Paul said, "I have been crucified with Christ; nevertheless I live; yet not I, but Christ liveth in me." To be crucified is to be terminated and slain. Although Paul had been crucified with Christ, nevertheless he lived, yet not Paul, but Christ. This "nevertheless...yet...but" is the Christian life.

THE NEED FOR TWO LIVES

The mystery of the Christian life is related to the fact that both Christ and we have two lives, the divine life and the human life. Christ was God, but one day He became man. As God, He had the divine life; as man, He had the human life. Thus, Jesus was the God-man, a Person with both the divine life and the human life. Was God's intention that Christ live out the human life or the divine life? The answer is that God intended Christ to live out the divine life in His human life. It will help us to understand this if we ask another question: Did God intend Christ to express His humanity or His divinity? The answer to this question is that God wanted Christ to express divinity in His humanity by means of the divine life. God can only be expressed by the divine life. For example, a cat cannot express a bird, for a bird can only be expressed by the life of a bird. In like manner, the human life cannot express God. To expect God to be expressed by the human life is like expecting a bird to be expressed by a cat. A cat cannot possibly express a bird because it does not have the life of a bird. Likewise, a man cannot express God if he does not have God's life. God's intention was that Christ would express Him by the divine life. Nevertheless, God wants to have Himself expressed in man. If God is expressed only in Himself, He will not be satisfied. He loves man and wants to be expressed in man.

Once again, let us use the relationship between a husband and his wife as an illustration. Every husband wants to be expressed, not in himself, but in his wife. Thus, the secret of being a good wife is for the wife to be the expression of her husband. For example, I enjoy eating Mandarin dumplings. However, I do not like to say this. Instead, I prefer that my wife say it for me. This indicates I desire to be expressed by my wife. If she does not express me, I am disappointed and displeased. Just as a husband wants himself expressed, not in himself, but in his wife, so God desires to have Himself expressed, not in Himself, but in man. This is not my concept; it is the concept of the Bible, wherein the relationship between God and man is likened to that between a husband and wife. A wife needs to learn one secret: to know what is in the heart of her husband and express it. If your husband likes to eat Mandarin dumplings, do not simply tell others that he likes to eat them. Rather, you should say, "We like to eat Mandarin dumplings." This will be most pleasing to your husband. Whenever my wife says this, my heart leaps for joy. This shows how much I desire to be expressed through her. In like manner, God wants to express Himself in man.

For the expression of God in man, two lives are needed, one life to express Him and another life to be the channel for this expression. This means that one life is needed to express God and another to be the channel. When some hear this, they may say, "This is not logical, for to express is to be the channel, and to be the channel is to express." Nevertheless, there is a difference here. It is impossible for man's life to express God, just as it is impossible for the life of a cat to express a bird. Only the divine life, God's life, can express God. Nevertheless, God desires that this expression be in man. Although the human life cannot express God, the human life is needed for the accomplishment of this expression. As we have pointed out, the Lord Jesus had two lives, the divine life and the human life. The divine life expressed God, and the human life accomplished the expression of God.

We have seen that only the divine life is able to express God. We have also seen that God does not want Himself expressed in Himself, but in man. When the Lord Jesus was on earth, everyone could see that He was a man. But very few realized that God was concealed within Him. God did not want Jesus to express Himself; He wanted Him to express God. Therefore, in order for Jesus to express God, He had to deny His human life by constantly putting it to death under the cross. In other words, He had to live a crucified life. Although He was always being crucified, nevertheless He lived, yet not He, but God. As Jesus lived the crucified life, this crucified life gave the opportunity for the divine life to be lived out for the expression of God. The power of Christ's resurrection needed the death that killed His natural life. The Lord Jesus had to place His natural life under death. When this took place, there was the opportunity for the divine life to rise up. In this we see the power of Christ's resurrection.

MISSING THE MARK

Concerning this matter of the power of Christ's resurrection, as in so many other matters, many Christians are missing the mark. When I was a child, the principal of the Southern Baptist elementary school I attended taught me to celebrate Easter by coloring eggs. Later, after I was saved and had begun to love the Lord, I was told to celebrate Easter by attending a sunrise service. Although Christianity may teach people to color Easter eggs or have sunrise services, it does not teach them concerning the power of Christ's resurrection. If we know the power of His resurrection, every meeting of the church will be a resurrection meeting and every day will be a resurrection day.

NOT IMITATION, BUT DISPENSATION

How glad I am to have two lives, the human life and the divine life! I was born of man to be a son of man. But I have also been born of God to be a son of God. Thus, I have a dual status, the status of a son of man and the status of a son of God. Although all real Christians have two lives, only the divine life can express God. Our natural human life is pitiful and cannot possibly express Him. Most of the sermons preached in the so-called churches teach people to use their human life to imitate the divine life. This is like teaching a monkey to act like a human being. Even if monkeys could act like humans, such behavior would not be genuine, but an imitation. Likewise, it is useless to teach people to imitate the divine life. In the Lord's recovery, we are not teaching people to do this. The goal of this ministry is not imitation, but dispensation. Our goal is to dispense something divine into you so that you may live by the divine life, the only life that can express God.

DECIDING TO BE CRUCIFIED

The one good aspect of the human life is that it is capable of making a decision whether or not to put the human life aside and to place it under the death of the cross. God cannot make this decision for us. We need to make it ourselves. When the Lord Jesus was on earth, God did not decide for Him that He should be crucified. As a human being, He Himself decided to put Himself daily under the cross. It is the same with us today. We need to decide whether or not we shall be crucified. We need to realize that we are good only to be crucified. If we are willing for this, we shall make a strong decision in favor of it. We shall say, "Brothers, if you want to crucify me, it is all right. I want to be crucified, terminated, placed under death." When we are willing for this and are placed into death, the crucified life will become the base for the resurrection life to rise up. Thus, by being crucified, we shall come to know the power of Christ's resurrection. But if we are not crucified, we cannot know the power of His resurrection. There is only one way for us to know the power of His resurrection, and that is to live a crucified life.

Often, brothers and sisters have told me about the problems they have in married life. Some have said, "Brother Lee, I have prayed about the situation, but the Lord has not answered my prayer. In fact, the more I pray, the worse the situation becomes. The situation is always the opposite of what I ask for in prayer." The reason for this is that so many brothers and sisters are not willing to be crucified. There is not always the need to pray so much. The Lord Jesus did not always pray as much as you do, but He was always willing to be crucified. He did not pray to the heavenly Father regarding the difficulties in His family, asking the Father to change His mother's disposition so that she would not be so troublesome to Him. Instead of praying like this, He was willing to be crucified, to put Himself under the death of the cross. Furthermore, although Peter caused the Lord Jesus considerable difficulty, the Lord did not send him away. Instead, He always put Himself under the death of the cross. Not only with Peter, but with all the disciples, the Lord Jesus continually put Himself aside. For example, the last time the Lord Jesus told His disciples that He was about to be crucified, none of them had an ear to hear this (Matt. 20:17-20). Immediately after the Lord spoke this word, they began to discuss among themselves who would be the greatest. If we had been the Lord Jesus, we would have rebuked them harshly for paying no attention to the word regarding crucifixion. But because the Lord Jesus was living a crucified life, He did not speak to them in this way.

THE WAY TO KNOW THE POWER OF CHRIST'S RESURRECTION

When the Lord put Himself under death, this death gave the best opportunity for the divine life within Him to come forth. Although He lived in the human life, He did not live out the human life. Instead, He lived out the divine life. The human life in Him was put to death, and His divine life was lived out. The result was the expression, not of Jesus of Nazareth, but of the very God, the divine Person within Him. This is the way to know the power of Christ's resurrection.

By the Lord's mercy and grace, we have come to know that the desire of God's heart is to express Himself through us. This expression, however, cannot be by our human life, but must be by the divine life within us. For this expression, we must be willing to put aside our human life. The Lord may give us certain helpers to assist us in this, a wife or husband, children, and the brothers and sisters in the church. Our environment helps us to be crucified. Nevertheless, we must be willing to be put under the death of the cross and to live a crucified life. This death will afford the opportunity for the divine life within us to be lived out. In this way we will know the power of resurrection. If we still preserve our natural life and pray that God will help us in certain matters, we are wrong. God will not answer the prayers to preserve our natural life, nor will He render any help to our natural life. Rather, He will say, "Don't pray for Me to help you. Go to the cross and remain there. If you are willing, I will help you to be put on the cross." This is what it means to live the crucified life.

In our family life and in the church life, we all need to go to the cross and remain there. The best way to know the power of Christ's resurrection in our married life is to go to the cross. The unique way is not to pray; it is to be crucified. This is true, not only in our family life, but even the more in the church life. To be a good brother or sister among the saints in the church life requires that we go to the cross to be crucified. Do not pray for God to change others. God will never answer such a prayer. Instead, go to the cross and remain there. This is the way that is according to His economy. If we are willing to go to the cross and stay there, we shall know the power of Christ's resurrection.

THE WAY TO MANIFEST THE DIVINE LIFE
AND TO DEFEAT THE ENEMY

If you read the four Gospels again in the light of this vision, the Gospels will all be new to you. You will see that they are a record of a crucified life. In nearly every chapter we find the Lord Jesus living under the cross. He lived this way for the release of the divine life. Because He lived a crucified life, He was never defeated. It is possible to defeat a living person, but not a crucified person. The best way to escape the attacks of the enemy is not to counterattack; it is to go to the cross. When Satan attacks you, go to the cross and remain there. That is all you need to do. Satan cannot defeat a crucified one. As we have seen, crucifixion affords a base for the power of Christ's resurrection to rise up that the divine life may be expressed. Thus, there is no need for us to counterattack. In fact, it will not always be necessary even to pray. What we need the most is to go to the cross and stay there to live a crucified life. If we do this, the divine life will be released and manifested. As long as we are willing to go to the cross and to remain there, everything will be in the power of resurrection. This is the way to know Christ and the power of His resurrection. This is not a matter of doctrine, but of experience. May the Lord give all of us the willingness and the determination to go to the cross and stay there that we may know the power of His resurrection.

Chapter Sixteen

TO KNOW THE FELLOWSHIP OF HIS SUFFERINGS

In the foregoing message we saw that the power of resurrection requires death as its base. If there is no death, it is impossible for the power of resurrection to be manifested. The four Gospels reveal this principle very clearly. The Gospels are a record of a Person who always lived under the death of the cross. Jesus was crucified not only at the end of the Gospels but throughout His life. As He was growing up and as He came into the ministry commissioned by God, He was continually under the death of the cross. In other words, He lived a crucified life. Based on the death of the cross, His resurrection power was manifested.

CHOOSING TO SET ASIDE THE HUMAN LIFE

The Lord Jesus had two kinds of life, the divine life and the human life. He had the divine life for the purpose of expressing God and the human life for the purpose of having God expressed in man. In order for Him to accomplish such a marvelous expression, He had to continually set aside His human life so that His divine life could be manifested. The Lord Jesus made the decision regarding the setting aside of His human life, not by His divine life, but by His human life. This decision had to be made by the Lord Jesus as a man, not as God. God had already decided that the human life should be set aside for the expression of the divine life. However, it was necessary for the man to agree with God's decision. Thank the Lord that, as a man, the Lord Jesus decided of His own free will to set aside His human life so that His divine life might be expressed.

This matter of the will brings us back to Genesis 2. When

God created man, He created him with a free will. The first man, Adam, was defeated; however, the second man, Jesus, came, also with a free will, and He was victorious. The entire universe, including Satan, the angels, and the demons, was watching to see what the Lord Jesus would do. Everything depended upon the decision He made with His will. Would He choose the will of God or something else? God's will was that Christ use His free will to choose God's will. Hallelujah, He did choose God's will! In Gethsemane the Lord prayed, "Not as I will, but as You will" (Matt. 26:39). To deny our will and to choose God's will means that we die on the cross.

Christ's commission was to express God in man. For this, He needed two kinds of life. In order to express God, He needed the divine life; and in order to express God in man, He needed the human life. As a man desiring to express God in His humanity, the first thing He had to do was to put His human life aside. This decision was not easy to make. Let me use once again the illustration of married life. Some sisters are eager to get married. But every sister who gets married must be prepared to be killed. The reason there are so many separations and divorces is that the wives are not willing to be killed by their husbands. Instead, they want to be emancipated. From the very beginning of her marriage, a sister must determine to take her husband's will. In every culture a bride wears a head covering during the wedding ceremony. This indicates the bride's submission to the will of her husband. For a wife to submit to her husband's will requires that she put herself to death.

When the Lord Jesus was about to begin His ministry, He was baptized. Baptism signifies burial, termination. Being buried in baptism was the inauguration of the Lord's ministry. During the three and a half years of His ministry, the Lord lived as a crucified and buried person, living always under death. This experience of death was the base for the manifestation of the power of resurrection. Where death was, there was resurrection.

For the sisters, marriage also is a form of baptism, a kind of burial. Forty years ago, I used to give a pleasant word at wedding meetings. But now if I am asked to say something,

I tell the couple that marriage is an altar upon which they will be slaughtered. Sisters, do not forget that to be married is to be buried. If you want to get married, you must be ready to be buried. If you realize this, you will have a happy married life, for your marriage will be in resurrection.

In marriage, God requires more of the wife than He does of the husband. God does not ask the man to be killed by his wife because in marriage the man represents God. God is the universal man, the universal husband. In a marriage the husband represents God as the universal husband. If the wives are willing to be buried and to live a married life that is under the killing of the cross, the power of resurrection will be manifested, and all the troubles will disappear. I can assure the sisters that Satan, the evil angels, and the demons will be terrified by their termination and burial and will not bother them. The reason you are bothered by so many things is that you are still so alive.

DEATH AND RESURRECTION

As we have pointed out, the first thing the Lord Jesus did when He came out to minister was to be buried by John the Baptist. This indicates that He exercised His will to terminate His natural life. When John the Baptist wanted to hinder Him from being baptized, the Lord seemed to say, "No, I must be baptized. You must put Me into the water." By being baptized by John, the Lord indicated that He was willing to put away His human life and to keep it always under the cross. For this reason, in the four Gospels we see a crucified and resurrected life. To repeat, the Lord was crucified and resurrected, not only at the end of the four Gospels, but at the beginning. Eventually the time came for the Lord to be crucified physically. Then, after this consummate death there was the ultimate resurrection. Thus, wherever death is, there is resurrection.

How much the power of resurrection can be manifested in us depends upon how much death we enter into. If we do not get into death at all, there will be no resurrection. If we have a little experience of death, a little of the power of resurrection will be manifested. The basic principle is this:

the more death, the more resurrection. In Philippians 3 Paul wanted to gain Christ and be found in Him in a condition of not having his own righteousness, but of living out God as his righteousness. He wanted to know Christ and the power of His resurrection by putting himself aside and living under the death of Christ. The result of living under Christ's death is knowing the power of His resurrection.

THE SPIRIT BEING THE POWER OF RESURRECTION

It is difficult to say what the power of resurrection is. Speaking of Christ, Paul says in Romans 1:4 that He was "designated the Son of God in power according to the Spirit of holiness out of the resurrection of the dead." Here Paul says that Christ was designated the Son of God in power according to the Spirit. This indicates that power is according to the Spirit out of resurrection. This proves that the power of resurrection is the Spirit. The Spirit is the reality of the power of resurrection.

In a previous message we pointed out that the Spirit is what remains after we set ourselves aside. If unbelievers set themselves aside, nothing will remain, for they do not have the Spirit as the remainder in them. We are different. If we put ourselves aside, we have the Spirit as the remainder within us. What is set aside is the self, and what remains is the Spirit. If a brother will set himself aside when his wife is arguing with him, the Spirit will come out. This is the power of resurrection. We need to do only one thing—always put ourselves aside. To do this is to put the self under death and to keep it on the cross. When we do this, we live a crucified life and have a base for the power of resurrection to be manifested.

EXPERIENCING RESURRECTION
BY SETTING OURSELVES ASIDE

Christian teachers have been talking about the Holy Spirit for centuries. Nevertheless, it is difficult for anyone to define the Holy Spirit. According to practical experience, not theology, the Holy Spirit is what remains after we put ourselves aside. The Holy Spirit that remains in us is unlimited.

Sometimes young sisters have told me, "Brother Lee, you have a great deal of the Holy Spirit. But the young sisters have very little of the Spirit." It does not matter whether you have much of the Spirit or little. What matters is that you have Him. As long as you have the Spirit, there is no limitation. However, the Spirit may seem limited if we are not willing to put ourselves aside.

A number of times sisters have come to me in tears. On the one hand, I felt sympathetic toward them. But on the other hand, I would not sympathize with them. They were crying because their environment was difficult or even unbearable, but they forgot about the Spirit. If they would be willing to put themselves aside, they would not shed so many tears. Rather, they would immediately be happy in the Lord. But if we are not willing to set ourselves aside, take up the cross, and put ourselves under death, the Holy Spirit will seem limited in our experience. Sisters, you have a spiritual checking account with unlimited savings. Because you have such an account, you can write a check to cover any situation. The way to write a check is to put yourself to death and, through death, to enter into the Spirit as the reality of resurrection. Whenever you find yourself in a difficult situation, do not weep or pity yourself. Instead, put yourself aside and keep yourself under the cross. Then spontaneously resurrection will be manifested in you, and you will be able to sing with joy these lines from a hymn by A.B. Simpson:

> 'Tis not hard to die with Christ
> When His risen life we know;
> 'Tis not hard to share His suff'rings
> When our hearts with joy o'erflow.
> In His resurrection power
> He has come to dwell in me,
> And my heart is gladly going
>   All the way to Calvary.

If we set ourselves aside, this will be our experience. There is no need for us to endeavor to go to Calvary. Rather, we simply need to exercise our will to decide to put ourselves aside. When the circumstances are difficult, do not feel sorry for yourself, but take up the cross and remain under the death of the cross. Then you will discover that where death is, there the power of resurrection is also. Immediately the Spirit, the power of resurrection, will rise up within you, and you will sing with joy, "'Tis not hard to die with Christ." You will find yourself glad to go all the way to Calvary. This is the Christian life. The more we go to Calvary, the more of the power of Christ's resurrection will be manifested. The more we know the power of His resurrection, the more we shall be happy to go to Calvary. This is a cycle. It is not a form of suicide; it is an enjoyment of resurrection power. We enjoy going to Calvary, and we enjoy the power of Christ's resurrection, the Spirit of holiness. This is the reality of the power of resurrection.

Today's Christianity is far away from this mark. For this reason, we are fighting, not against anyone or against any doctrine, but against religion. The battle today is between Christ and religion. The Lord's recovery is a matter of the living Christ, not a doctrinal Christ, a Christ in theory or theology. The Christ who is the reality of the power of resurrection is the life-giving Spirit. The Lord's recovery is for such a Spirit, but Christianity is for religion. In order to experience Christ, we must go all the way to Calvary. At Calvary there is a wonderful death, a death that brings in resurrection. After we have put the self on the cross, what remains will be the Holy Spirit. With this remainder we shall sense the power of resurrection. This is the power of Christ's resurrection. Like A. B. Simpson, we shall go all the way to Calvary, not sorrowfully and with weeping, but joyfully and with singing. We shall enjoy death through the power of resurrection.

SUFFERING FOR PRODUCING
AND BUILDING UP THE BODY

We go on from the power of resurrection to the fellowship of Christ's sufferings. Although it is wonderful to enjoy the power of Christ's resurrection, the power of resurrection is not mainly for our enjoyment. In God's economy there is no selfish enjoyment. The power of Christ's resurrection is for the producing and the building up of the Body. God's intention is not to express Himself through certain individuals; it is to express Himself through a Body composed of many believers. Thus, the expression of God in man is not an individual matter, but a corporate matter. If we put ourselves aside and remain under the death of the cross, we shall enjoy the power of resurrection. Immediately, the power of resurrection will produce the Body. This goal of producing and building up the Body stirs up opposition. Satan knows of this goal, and he stirs up opposition against it. The goal of building the Body always arouses opposition. When the opposition comes, we suffer. In this way we enter into the fellowship of Christ's sufferings.

Philippians 3:10 speaks of knowing Christ, of knowing the power of His resurrection, and then of knowing the fellowship of His sufferings. According to Colossians 1:24, these sufferings are for the Body. In this verse Paul says, "Who now rejoice in my sufferings for you, and fill up what is lacking of the sufferings of Christ in my flesh for his body's sake, which is the church" (Gk.). When I was young, I was troubled by this verse. I said, "Christ's sufferings have been completed. How can Paul say that there was something lacking in Christ's sufferings?" I honestly thought that Paul was wrong. How can we say that anything related to Christ is not complete? Nevertheless, the Bible reveals that there is something lacking in the sufferings of Christ. Although everything else related to Christ is complete, His sufferings are not complete.

CHRIST SUFFERING FOR REDEMPTION
AND FOR THE BODY

Christ's sufferings have accomplished two things. First, His sufferings have accomplished redemption. Without suffering, Christ could not redeem us. Second, His sufferings have also accomplished the producing and building up of the church. Thus, within His great sufferings, there is a part for redemption and a part for the producing and building up of the church. The Lord Jesus was on the cross for six hours. Strictly speaking, only the last three hours of His suffering on the cross were for redemption. During these hours, Christ became sin in the eyes of God (2 Cor. 5:21), for God gathered all of man's sin, placed it upon Him, and condemned Him. That was the reason the Lord cried out, "My God, My God, why have You forsaken Me?" (Matt. 27:46). Before He went to the cross, the Lord Jesus said that He was not alone because the Father was with Him (John 16:32). But when He was made sin, He suffered God's judgment and condemnation. This was Christ's greatest suffering, and through it He accomplished redemption. It is impossible for us to share in this aspect of Christ's sufferings. If we say that we can share in this aspect, we blaspheme. He alone suffered God's judgment on the cross for the accomplishment of redemption.

However, Christ suffered not only for redemption, but also for the producing of the Body. In the Gospel of John Christ is described as the Lamb of God who takes away the sin of the world (John 1:29). But He is also presented as the grain of wheat that fell into the earth to produce many grains (John 12:24). The Lamb suffered for redemption, whereas the grain suffered for reproducing. Although we cannot share in Christ's sufferings for redemption, we can share in His sufferings for reproducing and for building up the Body. Christ was the one grain, and we are the many grains. As the many grains, we must suffer in the same way the one grain suffered. The one grain did not complete all the sufferings that are needed for the building up of the Body. For this, there is something lacking, and the lack must be made up by you and me. There is a portion for each of us to make up.

When we put ourselves aside and remain under the cross, the power of resurrection will be our portion. Immediately opposition will rise up against us, and we shall suffer. This suffering is in the fellowship of the sufferings of Christ for the building up of the Body.

TWO KINDS OF SUFFERINGS

At this point we need to differentiate between two kinds of sufferings, the sufferings of Christ and the sufferings that come from our mistakes. Do not think that all the sufferings you undergo are for the building up of the Body. For example, you may suffer because you make a mistake in driving. Perhaps you make a wrong turn and go several miles out of the way, and this causes you to suffer. This suffering, however, is the result of a mistake or carelessness; it is not the suffering of Christ for the producing of the Body. Likewise, if you make an error in your financial records and find yourself several hundred dollars in debt, that is also the suffering caused by error, not the suffering Christ. However, suppose on your job you enjoy the power of Christ's resurrection. Because of this certain of your superiors oppose you, either passing you up for a promotion or causing you to be dismissed from your job. This suffering may be counted as the suffering of Christ for the producing and building up of the Body. Thus, one category of suffering is due to our mistakes and wrongdoings, and the other results from our testimony.

When we set ourselves aside and experience the power of resurrection, our testimony will be very strong. This will arouse the opposition of the enemy, and we shall suffer. This kind of suffering is the suffering of Christ. We all need to know the fellowship of Christ's sufferings, the sufferings that make up what is lacking of Christ's sufferings for the building up of the Body. This should be not merely doctrine, but an experience in which we enjoy Christ.

CHRIST LIVING HIS LIFE IN US

The Gospels reveal that the Lord Jesus was always suffering opposition. In suffering opposition, we experience Christ and enjoy Christ. By experiencing and enjoying Him in this way, we come to know Him experientially. The more we pass through death, the more Christ's resurrection power becomes our enjoyment; and the more we have the enjoyment of resurrection power, the more we know Christ by our experience. In other words, the very Christ whose life is recorded in the four Gospels lives His life again in us and in the same way. Therefore, we know Him, the power of His resurrection, and the fellowship of His sufferings. The Christ revealed in the Gospels becomes our experience, and we follow in His footsteps as He repeats His life in us. Because He repeats His life in us, we become one with Him in His steps. We follow Him by enjoying Him and by being one with Him. This means that we even follow Him in His suffering life. How wonderful this is! If you read the book of Acts again, you will see that Peter, James, John, Paul, and all the apostles were such people. The Christ revealed in the Gospels was lived out again in Acts. In the Gospels, Christ lived out Himself in Jesus; in Acts, He lived out Himself in the apostles; and now He intends to live out Himself in us.

KNOWING CHRIST EXPERIENTIALLY

We should know Christ not only by revelation, thus having the excellency of the knowledge of Christ. We need to know Him also by enjoying Him, by experiencing Him, by being one with Him, and by having Him live within us and walk with us. In this way we know Him not merely in an objective way, but much more in a subjective way. Thus, we know Him both by revelation and by experience. Eventually, He becomes us and we become Him. This enables us to say with Paul, "To me to live is Christ" (Phil. 1:21). We shall also be able to say that Christ is being magnified in us. This is the book of Philippians. This book reveals how to know Christ in an experiential way. It tells how to know Him, the power of His resurrection, and the fellowship of His sufferings. As we know Him in this way, we can say, "Christ is being magnified in me. For to me to live is Christ." Then we shall go on to say, "Oh, that I may gain Christ and be found in Him!" Eventually, as we shall see in a forthcoming message, we shall be able to say, "I can do all things in Him who empowers me" (Phil. 4:13, Gk.).

Chapter Seventeen

BEING CONFORMED TO HIS DEATH

We have seen that on account of the excellency of the knowledge of Christ, we should count all things loss that we may gain Christ and be found in Him, not having our own righteousness out from the law, but the righteousness that is God Himself lived out of us (Phil. 3:7-9). The purpose of this is that we might know Him, the power of His resurrection, and the fellowship of His sufferings. But Paul does not stop here; he continues by saying, "Being conformed unto his death" (v. 10). The excellency of the knowledge of Christ, the counting loss of all things, the gaining of Christ, being found in Him, knowing Him, knowing the power of His resurrection, and knowing the fellowship of His sufferings all issue in one thing—being conformed to His death. Thus, the burden in this message is to consider this matter.

CHRIST'S DEATH BEING A MOLD

In Philippians 3 the Apostle Paul considered the death of Christ to be a model, a form, or a mold. For example, when the sisters make cakes or cookies, they put the dough into a mold. By being pressed into the mold, the dough eventually is conformed to the shape of the mold. This is precisely Paul's meaning here. He regards the death of Christ as a mold and us as the dough to be put into the mold and pressed. The result is that we are conformed to the death of Christ.

CHRIST'S DEATH SYMBOLIZED BY BAPTISM

The death of Adam is terrible, and we loathe it. The death of Christ, however, is precious and lovable, and we all should treasure it. According to the Bible, the wonderful death of Christ is symbolized by baptism. In the Gospels the Lord

Jesus experienced two baptisms: the first at the beginning of His ministry, when He was baptized in water by John, and the second at the end of His ministry, when He was baptized on the cross. Both baptisms symbolize the lovable death of Christ.

Baptism signifies both burial and resurrection. When a person is baptized in water, he is buried. A person who believes in the Lord Jesus comes to realize that he is dead and needs to be buried. Thus, we bury him by baptizing him in water. However, we do not leave him there. After burying him, we immediately raise him up. Burying signifies termination, and being raised up signifies germination. Thus, baptism clearly has two meanings: burial, signifying termination, and resurrection, signifying germination. This is the profound significance of baptism in the Scriptures.

The Lord Jesus passed through two baptisms. In the eyes of God, to be baptized like this is the highest righteousness. According to God, righteousness means to be right according to God's commandments. In the Old Testament times, God gave His people ten commandments. If anyone kept these commandments, he would be right before God, and God's righteousness would be with him. If anyone broke a commandment, he had to present a trespass offering in order to be brought back to the right position and to maintain his righteousness before God. Moses came with two tablets of commandments and charged the people to keep the commandments so that they might be right with God and have the righteousness required by God according to His law. But John the Baptist came and told people that they had to be baptized. By this we see that with John the dispensation was changed. God's economy in the New Testament is different from that in the Old Testament. According to God's economy in the Old Testament, His people were required to keep the law in order to be righteous in His sight. But in the New Testament God does not require us to keep the commandments of the law; rather, He has ordained that we be buried. This means that He requires that we be terminated and germinated. This is God's New Testament ordination. If anyone in the New Testament economy keeps the ten commandments but refuses to be baptized, he is a rebel against God's ordination. Therefore, in the New Testament the highest righteousness is to be baptized.

THE HIGHEST RIGHTEOUSNESS

This is the reason that in Matthew 3 the Lord Jesus said that He had to be baptized in order to fulfill all righteousness (Matt. 3:15). When I read this portion of the Word as a young man, I was troubled by it. I could not understand why Jesus, the Son of God, had to do something to fulfill all righteousness. It seemed to be that He was already perfect and complete and did not need to be baptized. In His New Testament economy, God wants us to be terminated in order that we might receive the One who will germinate us. In other words, in the New Testament the righteousness God requires is that we live, not by ourselves, but by God.

Once again we may use married life as an illustration. Suppose a wife keeps her husband's commandments and does everything according to them. She does whatever her husband tells her. Although such a wife may be a good wife, she is not a sweet wife. The sweetest wife is the one who not only keeps her husband's word, but also lives by his life. There is a vast difference between these two things. However, it seems impossible for a wife to live by her husband's life because he cannot get into her to be her life. But our divine Husband, the Lord Jesus, has come into us to be our life. In the New Testament God does not command us to do this and that. Rather, He simply commands us to live by Him. Moses came with God's commandments, but Jesus Christ came with God Himself. Thus, the only thing God wants is for us to live by Him.

Living by God requires that we be killed. If we are still living, it is impossible for us to live by the life of another person. Some wives are very good in a legal way and do whatever their husbands say. But often these legally good wives have a judgmental attitude toward their husbands. The best wife is one who lives in the person of her husband, according to the very heart and desire of her husband. Such a wife does not live or act on her own, but lives and acts in and by her husband. Even though her husband cannot actually get into her and be her life, she still lives by him. The wife who lives like this is a sweet, lovely wife.

In the Old Testament, God sent Moses with ten commandments to the people. But in the New Testament God sent His Son to put Himself into His people so that they might live, not by themselves, but by God. Such a living is the highest righteousness, the righteousness required for entering into the kingdom of the heavens, the righteousness which surpasses that of the Pharisees, the righteousness which is according to God's law (Matt. 5:20). This righteousness surpasses the righteousness of the Pharisees because it is according to God Himself. In fact, it is even God Himself lived out of us.

The Lord Jesus took the lead to live this kind of life, living not by Himself, but by God. Therefore, when He came out to minister, the first thing He did was to go to John the Baptist to observe God's ordination to be terminated in baptism. This was a symbol of His death, the termination of His human life. His death terminated His human life so that the divine life might rise up in Him. In all the years He was on earth, he lived, behaved, acted, and moved by God and not by Himself. In baptism He buried His human life and was resurrected in the divine life. Thus, He was a person who kept His human life under the death of the baptism that buried his human life and resurrected Him in the divine life. In this matter the Lord Jesus did not live according to the law; He lived by God Himself. In John 6:57 He said, "As the living Father sent Me, and I live because of the Father, so he who eats Me shall also live because of Me." This is not a matter of conduct according to laws and regulations; it is a matter of living by Christ. To live this way means that we are in the model of Christ's death.

CONFORMED TO THE MOLD OF CHRIST'S DEATH

The Lord Jesus had a human life. Nevertheless, in answering God's ordination, He did not live by His human life, but by God Himself. Instead of keeping the law, He lived by God, not caring for requirements, regulations, or commandments, but only for God Himself. The Lord Jesus did not live merely according to His Father's commandments; He lived according to the Father Himself. Living such a life requires us to be terminated. This is the model, the mold, of Christ's death to which we are being conformed.

If we see this, we shall realize how far off the mark most of today's Christians are. Most of them are still in the Old Testament economy, under God's former ordination. But in the New Testament we should not be under that old ordination, but under the new ordination, the ordination of living not by ourselves, but by Christ. As long as we live by Christ, whatever we do and wherever we go is all right, because it is actually not we who are doing a certain thing or going to a particular place, but Christ who lives in us. In the past many of us thought that to be a Christian was simply to do whatever God asked us to do. But this is the Old Testament economy, not the New Testament economy. In the New Testament economy God does not ask us to do certain things, but to live by Him. Acting according to God's commandments does not require us to die, for we are needed to do something. But living by God requires us to die, not to do anything. In one sense, God needs us, and in another sense, He does not need us. He does not need us to do anything, but He does need us to die. God only needs us to go to the cross and die. To learn this lesson do not go to a professor to be educated; go to John the Baptist to be terminated.

The Lord Jesus was no exception to this. When He came to John the Baptist, John at first declined to baptize Him. But the Lord said, "Permit it now, for in this way it is fitting for us to fulfill all righteousness" (Matt. 3:15). The Lord Jesus had to be buried and raised up by God so that He might live no longer by Himself, but by God. This was the highest righteousness. For example, no wife is better than the one who lives by her husband, not by herself. This is what God desires today. He does not want us to do anything; He only wants us to die to our own life and to live out His life. This is the righteousness which is God Himself.

BURIAL AND RESURRECTION

Before His ministry began, the Lord Jesus passed through such a death. All the time He was on earth, He did not live by Himself. Rather, He always lived by the Father and said, "I can do nothing from Myself" (John 5:30). The Lord had been buried. How could a buried one do anything? Suppose you are buried. What would you be able to do? If you are still able to do something, it indicates that you have not been buried. Our status must be that of a terminated and buried person who can do nothing from himself. The Lord Jesus seemed to say, "I can do nothing from Myself. When I came out to minister, I was baptized, buried, under the water. Now, as a buried person, how can I do anything?"

Hallelujah, where burial is, there is resurrection! The burial is of the human life, and resurrection is of the divine life. Because He was buried and resurrected, the Lord Jesus did not live by His human life, but by the divine life. The Lord Jesus did everything by the Father who lived within Him (John 14:10), living as One who had been buried. Thus, the power of resurrection was always with Him.

At the end of His ministry, the Lord Jesus physically died on the cross. When the two sons of Zebedee came to Him seeking for a position, He said, "Ye know not what ye ask: can ye drink of the cup that I drink of? and be baptized with the baptism that I am baptized with?" (Mark 10:38). When they said to Him, "We can," Jesus said, "Ye shall indeed drink of the cup that I drink of; and with the baptism that I am baptized withal shall ye be baptized" (Mark 10:39). In the book of Acts we see that the apostles were in fact baptized in this way. They were all buried and resurrected. For example, in Acts Peter did not live by his human life, but by the divine life. He was under the death of Christ and was being conformed to it.

BECOMING THE LIFE-GIVING SPIRIT

We have seen that at the end of His life, the Lord Jesus literally entered into death and was buried. But after His physical burial, in which He was absolutely and thoroughly terminated, He was bodily resurrected. By His resurrection the divine life within Him was fully released. Hence, He became the life-giving Spirit (1 Cor. 15:45). As the life-giving Spirit, He entered into the disciples and infused them with

His life, the life that lived always under the death of the cross. This enabled the disciples to live in the form, in the model, in the mold, of the death of Christ. Thus, the Apostle Paul could declare, "I have been crucified with Christ; nevertheless I live; yet not I, but Christ lives in me" (Gal. 2:20, Gk.). Paul lived, not by his own life, but by Christ as his life.

THE DIFFERENCE BETWEEN LIVING AND DOING

It is important to see the difference between doing something and dying that we may live Christ. Doing things is according to the old ordination, but dying to live Christ is according to the new ordination. As we have seen, God today does not want us to do anything; He only wants us to die that we may live Christ. This is what it means to be conformed to Christ's death. This vision needs to control us. For example, as you are about to love someone, you need to consider whether you are loving by your self or by Christ. The same is true with the preaching of the gospel. Do you preach the gospel by your self or by Christ? God does not want you to preach the gospel in your self; He wants you to preach the gospel by Christ. You need to be able to say, "It is not I who preach the gospel; it is Christ." We need to live a life under the death of Christ until the redemption of our body, until we are literally and thoroughly terminated and enter into resurrection with the divine life. Until that happens, we must live in the principle of having our human life buried so that we may live by the divine life, which is Christ Himself. To do this is to be conformed to the death of Christ.

We are all in the process of being conformed to the death of Christ. Christ's death is the model, the form, for our daily living. Our very being needs to be conformed to His death. This means that our human life is always under death so that we no longer have our being according to our human life, but according to Christ.

THE TEMPTATION TO TURN FROM THE CRUCIFIED LIFE

As we are being conformed to Christ's death, temptations will come to induce us to live by ourselves instead of by the divine life within us. In John 12 the Lord Jesus faced such a temptation. After the resurrection of Lazarus, many Jews had come to believe in Him. The crowds that were in Jerusalem for the Passover heard of this miracle and even saw the resurrected Lazarus. When the Lord Jesus came to Jerusalem, He was given a warm welcome. The Pharisees even said that the whole world had gone after Him (John 12:19). Apparently, this was the golden time for the Lord Jesus, the man from Nazareth. Some Jews from Greece wanted to see Him. Not daring to approach Him directly, they asked Philip to speak to Him for them. When the Lord Jesus heard that they desired to see Him, He said, "Truly, truly, I say to you, unless a grain of wheat falls into the ground and dies, it abides alone; but if it dies, it bears much fruit" (John 12:24). The Lord Jesus was not excited by the warm reception given Him. Rather, He said that He would fall into the ground and die. He came to Jerusalem, not to be welcomed, but to die that many grains might be brought forth.

In John 12:25 the Lord Jesus said, "He who loves his life loses it, and he who hates his life in this world shall keep it unto eternal life." In the next verse He continued, "If anyone serves Me, let him follow Me; and where I am, there also shall My servant be." The Lord Jesus is in death, and all who want to serve Him must follow Him there. The Lord's emphasis was that we must always live, move, and act under death to terminate our human life so that we may be germinated with the divine life to live in the way God desires. This is the kind of life that we should live today. This is the highest righteousness.

Even the Lord Jesus was tempted to live according to His human life instead of according to the divine life. As we are in the process of being conformed to His death, we shall be tempted again and again to turn away from the crucified life. The temptations seek to induce us away from living a crucified life and to revert to living by our natural life. When we are tempted, we need to say, "I am no exception. Unless I die, I cannot bear fruit or release the divine life. Unless I die, I cannot live out Christ or say, 'To live is Christ.' I must keep myself always under the death of baptism and be conformed to Christ's death."

Being conformed to the death of Christ is the issue of all the foregoing items in Philippians 3. I am sorry that so few Christians have seen this. The more we have the excellency of the knowledge of Christ, the more we shall be conformed to His death. The more we count all things loss for Christ, the more we shall be conformed to His death. The more we know Him, the power of His resurrection, and the fellowship of His sufferings, the more we shall be conformed to His death. It is in being conformed to His death that we enjoy Christ, the divine life, and live out God as our righteousness. This is the way to experience Christ.

CHAPTER EIGHTEEN

THE ALL-ACCOMPLISHING DEATH

In Philippians 3:10 we see that Paul desired to be conformed to Christ's death. In verse 11 he speaks of the out-resurrection from among the dead (Gk.). In these two verses death and resurrection are covered. The death spoken of in verse 10 is not a negative death, the death of Adam, but a positive, lovable death, the death of Christ the Savior. Furthermore, the resurrection in verse 11 is not the ordinary resurrection, but the extraordinary resurrection, the outstanding resurrection. Hence, Paul calls it the out-resurrection. Verses 8 through 11, which are one long sentence in Greek, issue in two things: the lovable death of Christ and the out-resurrection from among the dead.

In verse 8 Paul speaks of the excellency of the knowledge of Christ Jesus the Lord. In order to have the excellency of the knowledge of Christ, we need the vision, the revelation, of Christ. If we have the vision, we shall see that there is no comparison between Christ and the law. We shall also count all things loss that we may gain Christ and be found in Him in a condition of not having a righteousness that is out from ourselves, but the righteousness that is God Himself lived out of us. Then we shall know Christ experientially, and we shall also know the power of His resurrection and the fellowship of His sufferings. All this issues in the lovable death of Christ and in the out-resurrection from among the dead. Christians today do not know Christ's lovable death or the extraordinary resurrection in an adequate way. But in order to experience Christ adequately, we must know these things.

CHRIST'S DEATH HAVING MANY ASPECTS

In this message I would like to share with you concerning the all-accomplishing death of Christ. Christ's death is lovable because it has accomplished so much for us. Among Christians, mainly the redeeming aspect of Christ's death is preached. There is hardly any mention of any other aspect of Christ's death. But according to the New Testament, there is more than one aspect of His death. John 1:29 says, "Behold, the Lamb of God Who takes away the sin of the world!" This verse indicates that the Lamb of God, our Redeemer, would die on the cross to take away our sins. We believe in this, and we praise the Lord for it. In our hymnal we have many hymns on the subject of Christ's redeeming death. We believe strongly that Christ, the Lamb of God, died on the cross as our substitute to take away our sins. However, other aspects of Christ's death are also found in the Gospel of John.

In John 3:14 the Lord Jesus said to Nicodemus, "And as Moses lifted up the serpent in the wilderness, even so must the Son of Man be lifted up." The brass serpent had the form of a serpent, but not the poisonous nature of the serpent. According to the Lord's word, the brass serpent typified the Lord Himself. This means that He was to be lifted up on the cross just as the brass serpent was lifted up on the pole (Num. 21:8-9). Thus, the Gospel of John reveals that Christ was to die as the Lamb to take away our sins for redemption and also that He was to die in the form of a serpent to deal with the poison of the serpent in us. This aspect of Christ's death is related to sin. Having nothing to do with redemption, it deals with the poisonous nature of the serpent, Satan. It deals with the satanic nature in our being.

A third aspect of Christ's death is found in John 12:24: "Truly, truly, I say to you, unless a grain of wheat falls into the ground and dies, it abides alone; but if it dies, it bears much fruit." Regarding Christ's death, John uses three figures: the Lamb, the brass serpent, and the grain of wheat. The grain of wheat indicates the life-multiplying aspect of Christ's death. Therefore, we have the aspect of redemption, the aspect of removing the serpentine poison, and the aspect of the multiplication of the divine life. The grain of wheat that falls into the earth and dies multiplies the divine life. Because we are sinful, we need Christ as the Lamb. Because we have a serpentine nature, we need Him in the form of a serpent to destroy the nature of Satan in our being. However, if He merely takes away our sins and our serpentine nature without imparting anything into us, we are still empty. Hence, there is the need of the third aspect of Christ's death, the aspect that releases the life in Him into us. When our sins are taken away, when our serpentine nature is dealt with, and when the divine life is imparted into our being, we are no longer empty, no longer void. All this is the result of Christ's death. Because the death of Christ has so many aspects, we may describe it as the all-accomplishing death. Now we need to see in detail more of what Christ's death has accomplished for us.

THE RELEASE OF THE DIVINE LIFE

In addition to the accomplishment of redemption, Christ's death has accomplished twelve things for us. The first is that Christ's death releases the divine life. Consider a grain of wheat. If a grain of wheat is kept in a container, it will remain alone; nothing will happen to it. In order for the grain to multiply by having the life within it released, the grain must die. We have pointed out that in John 12 Christ had come to His golden time. He had performed a great miracle in raising Lazarus from the dead, and a large number of Jews believed in Him because of it. When He was about to enter Jerusalem, a huge crowd welcomed Him enthusiastically. Even the Pharisees felt that their opposition of Him had been in vain because the world was following Him (John 12:19). Every preacher in Christianity would enjoy having such a great following. However, the Lord Jesus was not excited by the reception given Him by the crowd. When Philip told Him that the Greeks were interested in seeing Him, He said, "Truly, truly, I say to you, unless a grain of wheat falls into the ground and dies, it abides alone; but if it dies, it bears much fruit." The Lord Jesus seemed to be saying,

"Philip, I don't care for this welcome. Instead, I am ready to fall into the ground and die."

If I had been Philip, I would have been very disappointed and I probably would have said, "Lord, I'm excited because this is Your golden time. For three and a half years, You have been rejected, opposed, despised, and persecuted. Now the crowds are welcoming You. Lazarus is here as a strong testimony, and everyone is convinced and subdued. Even the Greeks want to see You. But You are not excited. Instead, You speak of a grain of wheat falling into the ground and dying. What does this mean?"

THE NEED FOR LIFE

Yes, although there was a great crowd, the question we must ask is this: Is there anything of life in this crowd, in this great following? No, the life that was in the Lord as the grain of wheat had not yet been released and imparted into them. Thus, the Lord seemed to be saying, "I have life in Me, but it has not yet been released and imparted into them. I am the grain of wheat containing life, but the crowd does not have life. Only through death can the life that is in Me be released and imparted into them. Philip, there is no other way. You are excited by this welcome, by this large following. But I don't care for the excitement or for the following. I came that these people may have life. What is needed is not excitement or a welcome or a following. What is needed is for Me to die so that the life within Me can be released into them. Philip, even you need My death. Although you have been following Me for three and a half years, you still do not have My life within you. The divine life is concealed and confined in Me. I must fall into the earth and die so that it can be released to produce many grains. I am now the unique grain. But after My death, you all will become grains just like Me. Philip, don't be excited about this situation. What you need is life. You need Me to die so that you may have life."

THE LORD BEING STRAITENED

In Luke 12:50 the Lord Jesus said, "But I have a baptism to be baptized with; and how am I straitened till it be accomplished!" Very few Christians understand this verse. When the Lord Jesus came out to minister, He was baptized by John. But in this verse He said that He still had a baptism to undergo and that He was straitened until it was accomplished. The word "straitened" in this verse means compressed. While the Lord Jesus was in His humanity, He was compressed; He was in a strait, in a narrow place. This means that He was restricted and that there was no release for Him. Within Him was something unlimited, immeasurable, and eternal. This was the divine life. The divine life in Him was compressed, straitened, constrained, and confined. In other words, it was limited. This limitation could be removed only by the baptism of dying on the cross. Then the unlimited divine eternal life within the Lord Jesus could be released.

In 1933 Brother Nee gave me a book entitled *The Release of the Lord*. This book covered John 12:24 and Luke 12:50. I cannot express the great help I received through the reading of this book. The day I read that book I saw that the death of Christ was not only for redemption, but also for the release and the impartation of the divine life that was within Him. Not only did His death release the life of God from within Him; it also imparted it into us, making us grains of wheat just like Him. The Lord Jesus said that if a grain of wheat falls into the ground and dies, it will produce many grains. Certainly the many grains are the same as the one grain. Thus, we, the grains produced out of Christ's death, are the same as Christ. Hallelujah, He was the one grain, and we are the many grains!

One difference between the one grain and the many is that He was willing to fall into the ground, but we are not. Instead of falling into the ground to die, we like to be uplifted. However, if we are lifted up, there will be no multiplication. The only way for a grain to multiply is to fall into the ground and die. Otherwise, it will remain alone, perhaps alone in a high place. All genuine Christians are grains, but not many are willing to fall into the ground and die. Some years ago there were thousands of "Jesus people," but where are they now? There was a huge crowd, but there was very little life because few experienced the death of Christ.

CONFORMED TO CHRIST'S DEATH FOR THE RELEASE AND IMPARTATION OF LIFE

A stanza of a hymn in our hymnal says:

> When we see the ripened harvest
> Of the golden countryside,
> We may know that many seeds have
> Fallen to the earth and died.

Before there can be a harvest, many grains need to fall into the earth and die. But who is willing to die? Instead of dying, nearly everyone wants to receive glory. Thus, no life is imparted into others. It is easy to have a crowd, but difficult to impart life into others. To do this, we need to die. This is my burden in this message. In the Lord's recovery we do not need a crowd; we need the death that releases life. We need to experience this aspect of Christ's death.

To be conformed to Christ's death is the real and practical experience of Christ. To experience Christ to the uttermost is to die and be conformed to His death. In the conformity to Christ's death, we experience Christ in the release of His divine life. We should not be content with mere outward increase. We must care for how much life the new ones receive through our impartation, for how much life is infused into others through us. This infusion of life depends not on our ability, strength, or teaching; it depends on our being conformed to the death of Christ. We need to be conformed to His death so that the divine life within us may be released and imparted into others. Time will tell how much life we have imparted into others. We may be able to stir up people or excite them, but what counts is how much life is in them after a number of years.

Life lasts; it is enduring. Anything that does not last is not life. Rather, it is merely something of emotion or excitement. I repeat, the Lord Jesus was not happy to have a large crowd. He preferred to fall into the ground and die so that life could be imparted into others. He had a baptism to undergo, and He was compressed until it was accomplished. The Lord seemed to be saying, "I am compressed, limited, confined. The divine life in Me is eternal and immeasurable.

Yet, it is confined in the shell of My humanity. I need to pass through baptism to break the shell of My humanity so that the divine life within Me can be released." The principle is the same with us today. Apart from being conformed to Christ's death, there is no way to experience Him.

In today's Christianity there are many big revivals, and thousands, even millions, of people claim to have been saved. But where is the power of today's so-called church? There is so little power because there is so little life. It is difficult to tell a Christian from someone who is not a Christian. We must not repeat the history of Christianity. The only way for us not to be a part of Christianity is to die. We need to pray, "Lord, grant me the grace to be willing to die. Lord, I want to follow You. You said that wherever You are, there will Your servants be. Lord, since You are in death, we must be in death also." What a need there is for the release of the divine life from within us! For this, we all need to die. I have a baptism to be baptized with, and I am compressed until it is accomplished. I need to be released by death, by falling into the ground and dying. Hallelujah, Christ died! Through death, the one grain has become the many grains.

THE MULTIPLICATION OF LIFE

The Lord's death not only releases the divine life, but also multiplies it. I regret that through the years I have not adequately ministered life to you. Therefore, we are still short of life. This shortage of life is probably due to the fact that I have not died enough. Life comes out of death. The divine life is within us, but how much this life is multiplied depends upon how much death we undergo. The more death we experience, the more life will be released from us. Only death can bring about the multiplication of the divine life; power cannot do it. Today's Christians devote their attention to power instead of to life. But only the death of Christ can multiply life.

THE FATHER BEING GLORIFIED

Through the death of Christ the Father is glorified (John 12:28; 13:31). Christ's death glorified the Father because it released the divine life. The release of the divine life from within Jesus was the glorification of God. Glory is God released and expressed. Hence, whenever the divine life within us is released, God is glorified. The unique way to glorify God is to die. The more we are conformed to the death of Christ, the more we glorify the Father. Many Christians are taught that the way to glorify God is to behave themselves. However, the more you behave yourself, the more you receive the glory. You do not give any glory to God. The only way to glorify God is to be conformed to the death of Christ. Then spontaneously the divine life within us will be released, and God the Father, the source of this life, will be glorified.

THE SAVING OF THE SOUL

Another thing accomplished by the death of Christ is the saving of our soul (John 12:25). The only way to save our soul is to die. The more we die with Christ, the more we save our soul.

DRAWING PEOPLE TO CHRIST

Through the death of Christ people are drawn to Christ. After telling Philip that He would die as a grain of wheat falling into the ground, the Lord said, "And I, if I be lifted up from the earth, will draw all men to Myself" (John 12:32). The words "lifted up" refer to the Lord's death on the cross. Through His death the Lord would draw men to Himself. The real attraction is in the dying. When we die the death of Christ and are conformed to His death, we shall be a magnet drawing people to Christ. The death of Christ on the cross has a lovable attraction. Such an attracting, the proper attraction, is not a matter of stirring up people emotionally. It is an attraction that comes through the release of life. When people contact us, they should be influenced by the divine life and realize that there is something within us different from anything that is in the worldly people. There is something heavenly and divine within us. This is the crucified life with its attracting power. Every crucified person is a magnet. Wherever we are, we need to experience Christ in this way.

JUDGING THE WORLD

The death of Christ also judges the world. In John 12:31 the Lord Jesus said, "Now is the judgment of this world; now shall the ruler of this world be cast out." The world is a satanic system, a satanic organization. This satanic system can be judged only by the death of Christ. When Christ died on the cross, His death spontaneously judged the satanic system of the world organization.

CASTING OUT SATAN

Furthermore, according to John 12:31, the death of Christ casts out the ruler of this world. When Christ died on the cross, He cast out Satan. If we exercise our own strength to reject the world or to fight against the ruler of the world, we shall fail. The best way to overcome the world and to defeat Satan is to be conformed to the death of Christ. If we are willing to be conformed to His death, we shall be victorious over the world and Satan.

DESTROYING THE DEVIL

Hebrews 2:14 reveals that the death of Christ destroys the Devil. This verse says, "Since therefore the children have partaken of blood and flesh, He also Himself in like manner shared in the same, that through death He might destroy him who has the might of death, that is, the Devil." Through death, Christ destroyed not only the Devil, but also death. Since the one who held death has been destroyed, death has been destroyed also. This was accomplished through the death of Christ on the cross.

BLOTTING OUT THE ORDINANCES

Christ's death has also blotted out the ordinances (Col. 2:14). It is not an easy matter to give up ordinances. If we drop one ordinance, we immediately make another one. If there were no self or flesh, it would be impossible to have ordinances. Thus, the best way to blot out the ordinances is to crucify the flesh and the self. Every ordinance is established by the flesh or by the self. This indicates that the problem is not actually with the ordinances, but with the self and the flesh. By His death on the cross, Christ has blotted out all the ordinances that were according to the law. In order for the one new man to be created, the ordinances had to be blotted out (Eph. 2:15). However, few Christians realize this. That is the reason there are so many ordinances in today's Christianity. As the years go by, more and more ordinances are created by the self and by the flesh. We need to deal with the flesh and the self so that there will be no more ordinances. If we are conformed to the death of Christ, all the ordinances will be abolished.

STRIPPING OFF PRINCIPALITIES AND POWERS

By His all-accomplishing death, the Lord Jesus has stripped off principalities and powers (Col. 2:15, Gk.). The powers of darkness are related to our flesh. We may even say that they are wrapped up with our flesh and self. In the self there is Satan and the power of darkness. Do not argue that the powers of darkness are in the air. Yes, these powers are in the air, but they are also related to our self and our flesh. When the Lord Jesus was crucified, He nailed the flesh and the self on the cross. By doing that, He also stripped off the principalities and powers.

Suppose I am wearing a white shirt and that on this shirt are some spots of dirt. The best way to remove the dirt is to strip off the shirt. When the shirt is removed, the dirt is removed also. Our flesh and self are like the white shirt. God created this white shirt, but Satan has caused spots of dirt, the principalities and powers, to appear on it. The best way to eliminate these spots is to strip off the shirt, that is, to deal with the flesh and the self.

Let us once again use married life as an illustration. Brothers have often come to me with difficulties they are having with their wives. I have said to them, "The only way to deal with the problem is for you to go to the cross. Do not deal with your troublesome wife. Deal with the self that is bothered by her. She has a bothering self, and you have a bothered self. Instead of dealing with your wife's bothering self, deal with your bothered self. If you are buried in the tomb, you will not be troubled by your wife any more. The reason you are troubled by her is that your self is still so active. Your self wants to have a wonderful wife who has been dealt with by the Lord. But I will not take sides with you. I take sides with your wife in killing you so your self might be buried. Brother, if you are willing to be buried, there will be no problems."

The reason that Satan and the principalities and powers trouble you is that you are still wearing the "dirty shirt." If you strip off the "shirt" and leave it in the tomb, the evil powers will also be stripped off. It is in this way that Christ, by His death on the cross has stripped off all the principalities and powers. When He went to the cross in His flesh, all the principalities and powers followed Him. The Lord seemed to say, "Principalities and powers, follow Me. I am going to the cross. By My death on the cross, I shall strip you off." This is the meaning of Colossians 2:14 and 15.

CRUCIFYING THE OLD MAN

By His death, Christ has also crucified our old man (Rom. 6:6). Christ died not only for our sins, but also because of our self, which is our old man, our sinful old man. Sins are the expression of our old man, whereas our old man is the source of our sins. This old man has been crucified on the cross of Christ.

CRUCIFYING THE FLESH

When He was crucified on the cross, Christ also crucified our flesh with its passions and lusts (Gal. 5:24, Gk.).

The death of Christ has accomplished so many positive and negative things. Everything negative has been dealt with by the cross of Christ. This is the all-inclusive death, the all-accomplishing death. When we are conformed to such a death and are willing to undergo such a baptism, all the positive aspects of Christ's death will be realized, and all the negative things will be terminated. If we are willing to live under this death, there will be no problems.

Chapter Nineteen

ATTAINING UNTO THE OUT-RESURRECTION

Philippians 3:10 and 11 speak of both death and the out-resurrection from among the dead (Gk.). The death here is the lovable, all-accomlishing death of Christ. In the previous message we saw the many things that Christ's death has accomplished on our behalf. In this message we come to the result or the issue of being conformed to Christ's death: that we may attain unto the out-resurrection from among the dead. Death is the condition for our attaining to the out-resurrection. Hence, in these verses we have both the condition and the goal. The Greek word translated "attain" in verse 11 actually means "arrive at." This indicates that Paul desired to arrive at a certain goal, the goal of the out-resurrection.

THE GOAL OF THE CHRISTIAN LIFE

Many Christians are not clear about the goal of their Christian life. After we believed in the Lord Jesus according to God's New Testament economy, we were baptized. The significance of baptism is to terminate our natural being and to be germinated with the divine life. In baptism the natural life is buried, and a new life rises up. Baptism, however, is simply the beginning of our Christian life. Our Christian life also has a goal, and this goal is the out-resurrection. This term "out-resurrection" means that every part of our being will be resurrected. When we were baptized, our old life, our natural human life, was terminated and buried, and a new life, the divine life, which is Christ, rose up from within. At that time, we began our Christian life and walk. The Christian walk involves a long process, and it takes us a long way. At the end of this walk is the goal at which we need to arrive. As we have pointed out, this goal is the out-resurrection, the extraordinary resurrection. The way toward this goal is the process of resurrection.

On the day we were baptized, we should have realized that our old man, the natural man with the old life, was buried. Through that burial, the divine life, the eternal life, rose up within us, and our Christian walk began. A new life had come to live in us with the goal of bringing our whole being into resurrection. Between baptism and the goal there is the long process of arriving at the out-resurrection. Although our baptism signified that our old man had been buried and that another life had risen up to live in us, we did not live according to what was signified by our baptism. Most of the time we lived by our natural life, not by Christ. Because we still live so much by our natural life, the process of resurrection must continue.

The Epistle to the Philippians is composed in such a way that if we do not have experience, we shall have difficulty understanding it. Remember that verses 8 through 11 of chapter three are one long sentence. In verse 8 Paul says that he counts all things loss on account of the excellency of the knowledge of Christ Jesus the Lord. Furthermore, in verse 9 he tells us that he desires to be found in Christ in such a condition that he does not have his own righteousness out from the law, but that he has God Himself lived out of him as his righteousness. All this is for the purpose of experientially knowing Christ, the power of His resurrection, and the fellowship of His sufferings and also of being conformed to His death in order to arrive, by any means, at the out-resurrection from among the dead.

Arriving at the out-resurrection is the result, the issue, of being conformed to Christ's death. To be conformed, molded, to the death of Christ means that we remain always in His death. If we remain in Christ's death, allowing ourselves to be molded into its likeness, the outcome will be that every part of our being will be gradually resurrected.

THE MEANING OF THE OUT-RESURRECTION

Bible expositors have had a difficult time understanding

the word "resurrection" in Philippians 3:11. They have found it especially difficult to decide whether it refers to the future resurrection at the time of the Lord's coming back or to the experience of resurrection life today. Some have said that this resurrection cannot possibly refer to a present experience of resurrection, but must refer only to the resurrection at the time of the Lord's coming back when the dead saints will be raised up. Others, disagreeing with this view, have said that according to the context, it must refer to a present experience. During the years, I have spent a great deal of time praying about this and seeking for the Lord's understanding of it. I have come to see that this matter of the out-resurrection is a process that has a beginning and an ending. The time between the beginning and the ending is the period of the process. Thus, the out-resurrection spoken of in this verse does not refer strictly to something either present or future. Instead, it refers to the process that began on the day we were baptized and that will conclude when we arrive at the outstanding resurrection. As we move on toward the goal, we are in the process of being resurrected.

Our resurrection began with our regeneration. As sinners, we were all part of the old Adam. In every respect we were old. We were old in body, soul, and spirit. But when we believed in the Lord Jesus, something new entered into us. The Holy Spirit of God came in to regenerate us with the life of God. Thus, by regeneration, our old, deadened spirit was resurrected. The Bible says that when we were saved, we were quickened, made alive (Eph. 2:5). Before we were saved, we were dead in trespasses and sins (Eph. 2:1; Col. 2:13). But when we believed in the Lord Jesus, the Holy Spirit of God came in to quicken our deadened spirit with the divine life. At that time, part of our being, our spirit, was resurrected. But what about the other parts of our being, such as our mind, emotion, will, and heart? When we were regenerated in our spirit, these parts were not yet resurrected. Nevertheless, God's goal is to resurrect our whole being.

THE PROCESS OF RESURRECTION

Much of theology is too doctrinal and cannot be applied

to our experience. Theology may merely tell us that if a believer dies before the Lord Jesus comes back, he will eventually be resurrected from the grave. This, of course, is correct, but it is not a very practical teaching. The Bible reveals that, according to God's economy, we are first resurrected in our spirit. From that time onward, our Christian walk is a process of resurrection. Day by day, God is processing us from the natural life to the resurrected life. In Philippians 3:10 Paul spoke of being conformed to Christ's death. This is a continual process, not a once-for-all experience. As we know Him, the power of His resurrection, and the fellowship of His sufferings, we are under the process of being conformed to Christ's death.

Suppose a certain brother is baptized, realizing that his natural life is being buried and that he has been quickened by the divine life. From that time onward, he begins to walk toward the goal of having his entire being brought into resurrection. He loves the Lord and prays to the Lord with the expectation that eventually every part of him will be resurrected. He begins to have the excellency of the knowledge of Christ and, one by one, he begins to count things loss so that he may gain Christ and be found in Him in a condition of not having his own righteousness out from the law, but of having God Himself lived out of him as his righteousness. He also begins to experientially know Christ, the power of His resurrection, and the fellowship of His sufferings. Gradually, he also begins to be conformed to the death of Christ. As he seeks the Lord and experiences Him, he spontaneously realizes, item by item, the things in him that have been terminated. For example, one day he may come to see that his love for his wife should not be a natural love. Thus, he may pray, "Lord, I confess that my love for my wife has been a natural love. Grant me the grace to live a crucified life with my wife." This is to be conformed to Christ's death in the particular matter of loving his wife. Several days later he may realize that even his contact with the saints has been too natural. He has cared for the saints and tried to shepherd them, but even in his shepherding he has been too natural. Therefore, he prays and confesses this matter to the Lord, asking Him for the grace to no longer shepherd the saints according to his natural life. He may pray, "Lord, I want to be conformed to Your death. Like You, I want to live a crucified life. When You were on earth, You did not love people or care for them according to the natural life. Everything You did was in resurrection. Lord, grant me the grace that from now on I will not shepherd Your saints in my natural life, but in You." Through this experience, he becomes conformed to the death of Christ in this matter also. Item by item, he is conformed to Christ's death. The more he is conformed to Christ's death in this way, the more his being is resurrected. In loving his wife and in shepherding the saints, he is resurrected.

We need to point out that this process has nothing to do with the improvement of behavior. It is not something ethical or religious, but altogether a matter of transformation through the divine life, of having the natural life terminated and of being brought into the divine life.

PAUL'S EXPERIENCE

Let us now consider Paul's situation regarding this matter when he wrote the Epistle to the Philippians. Do you believe that he was thoroughly resurrected at that time? I do not believe this. At least a small percentage of his being must still have been natural; it was not yet Paul the Apostle, but still Saul of Tarsus. On the way to Damascus, he was enlightened and knocked down to the ground. On that day, he was saved, and his spirit was resurrected. Nevertheless, his whole being was not resurrected at that time. However, a great deal more of his being, probably more than ninety-five percent, had been resurrected. Because he was not fully in resurrection, he was still endeavoring to arrive at the out-resurrection from among the dead. He was still in the process.

RESURRECTED UNTO LIFE

My burden in this message is to point out to you that our Christian walk is a matter of death and resurrection. Today we are all on the way to the out-resurrection from among the dead. Paul desired to be conformed to Christ's death so that, by any means, he might arrive at the out-resurrection from among the dead. As we have pointed out, this does not refer merely to the resurrection of the dead in the future. The future resurrection of the dead will not be a resurrection unto life, but unto judgment. When the dead unbelievers are resurrected, they will be judged. The believers, however, are resurrected from among the dead. This is a resurrection, not unto judgment, but unto life. Thus, we are being resurrected, not for judgment, but for life. Day by day and little by little, we are being resurrected unto life. Every time I am resurrected a little more, I have more life. Each step of the process of the out-resurrection from among the dead is unto life. The Christian walk is not a matter of behavior or ethics; it is a process of resurrection. We are being processed into resurrection. We are all in this process, and we are all in resurrection. The difference between us is a matter of degree. For example, one brother may be fifty-five percent resurrected and another brother, forty-five percent.

BEING CONFORMED TO CHRIST'S DEATH

We need to forget the teachings about the improvement of behavior. Do not try to love others, to control your temper, or to be a good husband or wife. Instead, endeavor to be conformed to Christ's death. You may still be under the concept that you must improve your behavior. But the only thing you need to do is to be conformed to the death of Christ. I admit that this is much easier to say than it is to practice. In this matter, we need Christ to help us. I have no burden to help you control your temper or be a good wife or husband. My burden is to charge you to be conformed to the death of Christ. As you are about to love someone, be conformed to His death. As you are about to lose your temper, be conformed to His death. As you are about to go somewhere or do something, be conformed to His death. Simply be conformed to the death of Christ. Unbelievers cannot be conformed to Christ's death because they do not have the Holy Spirit within them. But because we have the Holy Spirit within us and because we have been regenerated with the divine life, we can be conformed to the death of Christ.

We need to see the vision that God's economy is not a matter of ethics or religion, but of being conformed to the death of Christ. This means that we need to be buried and remain always in death to be conformed to Christ's death. However, time after time, we come out of the tomb and thereby stop being conformed to Christ's death. Often we live and act in a natural way, even in doing spiritual things or scriptural things. We may act according to the Scriptures, but we are not conformed to the death of Christ in doing so. Rather, we are in our natural life. It is easy for Christians to give up evil things, but it is very difficult to be conformed to the death of Christ and not to do anything by our natural life. Nearly fifty years ago I gave up the sinful things, but I am still learning how to be conformed to Christ's death. We all were born natural, raised to be natural, and educated and trained to be natural. We are continually doing things in a natural way. This is why it is so difficult for us to drop the self. In so many things we are not yet resurrected.

MEETING CHRIST IN RESURRECTION

As long as we are not in resurrection, we cannot experience Christ, because Christ today is in resurrection. Even if you are a Christian, you cannot experience Christ if you remain in the natural life. But when you are willing to be conformed to Christ's death and are spontaneously brought into resurrection, you will meet Christ in resurrection. Here, in resurrection, Christ becomes our experience. Take being nice as an example. The sisters are usually very nice. This niceness, however, is natural. When some sisters hear this, they may decide to no longer be nice. But to do that is to be sinful. The way is neither to be nice nor to not be nice; it is to be conformed to the death of Christ. Whoever we are, whether we are young, middle-aged, or elderly, we all need to be conformed to the death of Christ. Even the teenagers need to be put into the mold of Christ's death and conformed to it. If we are not conformed to the death of Christ, we simply cannot experience Him.

In speaking of the resurrection in verse 11, Paul specifically speaks of the out-resurrection. This indicates that Paul wanted to be in the outstanding resurrection. He did not simply want to graduate; he wanted to be the valedictorian, an outstanding graduate. Paul desired this because he realized that by this outstanding resurrection he was experiencing Christ, was partaking of Him, and was enjoying Him. Here in this resurrection Christ was truly the life-giving Spirit to him.

In our daily living we need to learn to practice one thing: To check whether we are conformed to the death of Christ before doing anything. Do not say that a certain thing is good, scriptural, spiritual, or heavenly. The thing you plan to do may be very heavenly or spiritual, but in doing it you may not be heavenly or spiritual. It is not a matter of how we do a certain thing; it is a matter of who is doing it, we or Christ, the natural life or the resurrected life. Even singing a hymn to God is wrong if we sing it in the natural way. Our singing, and our praises also, must be in resurrection. Do not question whether something is good or bad, right or wrong. Instead, check whether or not you are conformed to the death of Christ in doing it. If you are being conformed to His death, you will be in resurrection, and in resurrection you will meet Christ, experience Christ, and enjoy Christ. Christ today is the life-giving Spirit in resurrection. If you are not in resurrection, you need to repent that you may be brought into resurrection. Then in resurrection you will meet Christ.

Because Christians do not realize this, they exert very little influence on the people around them. But a Christian who is in the process of resurrection should influence others. Today's Christians have so little influence. We, however, must not be a continuation of today's Christianity. We must be known by our experience of being conformed to Christ's death.

We need to forget everything ethical or religious and concentrate on practicing being conformed to the death of Christ, so that by any means we may attain to the out-resurrection from among the dead. I can testify that day after day I experience Christ and enjoy Christ in this way. This is the message of the book of Philippians.

We shall continue to be processed into resurrection until our whole being is resurrected. Then we shall simply need to wait for our body to be redeemed, that is, for our body to be resurrected. This was Paul's meaning in Philippians 3. He was in the process of being resurrected by being conformed to the death of Christ.

THE PRESENT EXPERIENCE OF RESURRECTION

Other verses prove that the out-resurrection spoken of in Philippians 3:11 is not merely a future event, but a present process. Romans 6:4 and 5 say that as we have been buried in the likeness of Christ's death, so we shall also walk in the newness of life. This means that we shall be resurrected in the likeness of His resurrection. This likeness is the newness of life.

Romans 8:10 and 11 say that we have Christ within us, that our body is dead because of sin, but that our spirit is life because of righteousness. Furthermore, the Spirit who raised up Christ from among the dead will give life to our mortal body so that our body may enjoy resurrection life. This is not only a future matter; it is the process of resurrection that we are undergoing today.

In 2 Corinthians 1:8 and 9 Paul said that he was pressed out of measure, beyond strength, and even despaired of life; he also said that he had the sentence of death upon him. Nevertheless, the God who raises the dead sustained him by the power of resurrection. In 2 Corinthians 4:10 Paul said that he was always bearing about in the body the putting to death of Jesus so that the life of Jesus might be made manifest in his body (Gk.). In verse 16 of the same chapter he said that the outward man is being consumed but the inward man is being renewed day by day. This is the process of the resurrection. We will continue in this process until we arrive at the goal of the out-resurrection. This is the way to experience Christ.

This word must not be mere doctrine to us; it is something that we need to practice in our daily living. In whatever we do we should ask whether or not we are being conformed to the death of Christ. We need to be conformed to His death so that by any means we may arrive at the out-resurrection from among the dead. This is the only way for the Lord to go on in His recovery, the only way for the Lord to build up His church, the only way for Him to prepare His Bride, and the only way for us to bring the Lord back. The unique way is to be conformed to the death of Christ so that we may attain unto the out-resurrection from among the dead.

Chapter Twenty

ONE THING TO DO

In Philippians 3:8-11 a number of matters are covered. Nevertheless, there is just one outstanding point—to be conformed to the death of Christ so that, by any means, we may attain unto the out-resurrection from among the dead. For this, we first need the excellency of the knowledge of Christ. By means of such an excellency, we shall be willing to count all things loss in order to gain Christ and be found in Him in a condition of not having our own righteousness out from the law, but having the righteousness that is God Himself lived out of us. Then we shall experientially know Christ, the power of His resurrection, and the fellowship of His sufferings. We shall also be conformed to His death in order to arrive at the out-resurrection from among the dead.

EXPERIENCING CHRIST
IN THE PROCESS OF RESURRECTION

Arriving at the out-resurrection means that our entire being has been gradually and continually resurrected. On the day the Spirit of God came into us to regenerate our spirit, the process of resurrection began. Firstly, God resurrected our deadened spirit. From that time onward, He has been working within us to resurrect every part of our being, our mind, emotion, and will. Eventually, even our body will be resurrected and transfigured. This means that we shall be fully resurrected out of our old being into the new creation. This is God's economy, God's intention, God's goal. Through this process Christ will be thoroughly wrought into us. It is in this way that we experience Christ.

Experiencing Christ is not merely a matter of enjoying His love, grace, or help. To experience Christ is to have Christ wrought into our being to resurrect us out of our old being into the new creation. When the New Jerusalem comes with the new heaven and the new earth, every part of our being will be a new creation. The way to become the new creation is to have our being processed in resurrection from the old creation to the new. All of us are partly resurrected. This means that another part is still unrenewed and yet remains in the old creation. Therefore, we are in the process of resurrection to be renewed from the old creation to the new creation. This process of resurrection enables us to participate in Christ and to partake of Christ. This is the experience of Christ.

The experience of Christ is not something so superficial as merely receiving grace, obtaining help, or enjoying love from the Christ in the heavens or from the Christ in us. To experience Christ is to be conformed to His death. In this death we are processed in resurrection from the old creation to the new creation. Eventually, the new creation will simply be Christ wrought into our being and enlarged in us.

OBTAINING THAT FOR WHICH WE HAVE BEEN OBTAINED

In verse 12 Paul says, "Not as that I have already attained, or have already been perfected: but I pursue, if also I may obtain that for which also I have been obtained of Christ Jesus" (Gk.). Here Paul seems to be saying, "I have not reached the goal. Rather, I am still in the process. Although I may be ahead of all of you, I have not yet attained, nor have I been perfected. I am still on the way." Although the Apostle Paul was very mature when he wrote the Epistle to the Philippians, he still said that he had not yet been perfected.

In verse 12 Paul says that he pursued in order to obtain that for which he had been obtained by Christ Jesus. This word is not easy to understand. When Paul was Saul of Tarsus, he was zealous for the law. He was zealous to such an extent that he even persecuted the church. The Greek word rendered "pursue" is also the word for persecute. Thus, when Saul of Tarsus was persecuting the church, he pursued it in a negative sense. On the way to Damascus, he suddenly saw a light from heaven, and he was knocked to the ground. Then he heard a voice saying, "Saul, Saul, why persecutest thou me?" (Acts 9:4). On that day Saul of Tarsus was obtained by Christ. He was obtained by Christ so that he might obtain Christ. Therefore, in Philippians 3:12 Paul seemed to be saying, "Christ has obtained me for the purpose of my obtaining Him. It was easy for Him to obtain me. By one action as I was on the road to Damascus, He thoroughly obtained me. But it takes a long time for me to obtain Him. From the day He obtained me, I have been doing my best to obtain Him. Throughout all the years since then, I have been obtaining Christ."

On the day we were saved we were obtained by Christ. He obtained us in order that we might obtain Him. How good it is to be obtained by Christ! Do you realize that even now He is embracing you so that you may obtain Him? To repeat, for Him to obtain us is easy. By one action He obtained us all. But our obtaining of Him is not once for all. Rather, it is an ongoing process. When I consider the situation among today's Christians, I am very disappointed. But when I consider the brothers and sisters in the churches, I am quite encouraged, for many of them have been obtaining Christ. Continually and gradually, daily and even hourly, we need to obtain more of Him. The more we obtain Him, the more we are resurrected. In other words, the more we obtain Christ, the more we are renewed and transformed from the old creation into the new creation. Because this is a continuing process, Paul said that he was still on the way to obtain Christ. He had not yet obtained everything of Christ.

Philippians 3:13 and 14 say, "Brethren, I count not myself to have obtained: but one thing I do, forgetting those things behind, and stretching forth unto those things before, I pursue toward the goal for the prize of the above calling of God in Christ Jesus" (Gk.). In these verses Paul seemed to be saying, "I have not yet reached the end of the process in God's economy, but I am pursuing toward the goal. When I was Saul of Tarsus, I pursued the church in a negative way. But now I am pursuing Christ in a positive way." Paul undoubtedly was of a very strong character, both when he was Saul of Tarsus and when he was Paul the Apostle. Being a strong character, he never did anything halfway. When he was Saul of Tarsus, he persecuted the church negatively, and after he became the Apostle Paul, he persecuted Christ positively.

OUR NEED TO PERSECUTE CHRIST

In order to experience Christ, in this sense we need to persecute Him. When some hear such a word, they may say, "It is heresy to say that we, the lovers of Christ, should persecute Him." Yes, we need to persecute Christ. We should say, "Lord Jesus, I don't care whether You are willing or unwilling, You must be for me. Even if You say that You are not ready for me to experience You, I shall persecute You to make You ready." When this is viewed in a positive sense, it is not too much of an extreme. Mary Magdalene was an example of one who persecuted the Lord Jesus in a positive way. Early in the morning on the day of His resurrection, she pursued Him. She persecuted the resurrected Christ and persuaded Him to do something that He was not willing to do. We all need to seek the Lord in such a way.

FORGETTING THE THINGS BEHIND

Have you ever persecuted the Lord Jesus in a positive way? Probably not. Have you ever sought the Lord by persecuting Him until He goes along with you? Whenever you persecute Him in such a positive way, you will forget the things behind. Only those who are lukewarm, who are neither cold nor hot in loving the Lord, consider the things of the past and remember their experiences of years ago. But when you persecute the Lord, you have no time to think about the past. Thus, the best way to forget the past is to be fully occupied with pursuing the Lord right now. If we are not occupied in this way, we shall be continually occupied with the things of the past, either positive things or negative things. We must be busy with pursuing Christ and persecuting Him in a positive way. If you get into the spirit of Paul, you will realize how busy he was in persecuting Jesus and in compelling Him to be his enjoyment. There was no room in his mind for considerations about the past. To repeat, to consider the past is a sign of being lukewarm. But when you are burning and are persecuting the Lord Jesus in a positive way, you have no room in your mind to think of the past. Instead, you are occupied with pursuing toward the goal.

THE GOAL AND THE PRIZE

Both the goal and the prize are Christ. Christ is within us, but He is also before us at the end of the race as the goal that we are striving to reach. To say that Christ is the goal means that He is the highest enjoyment. The Christ who is in us for our enjoyment today is not the goal. The goal is the highest enjoyment of Christ, that is, the out-resurrection. No matter how much we experience Christ today, we have not yet reached the goal of the highest enjoyment of Christ. This experience of Christ is still before us. As soon as we reach the goal, the goal will immediately become the prize. When you obtain the prize, you may shout with the enjoyment of the highest experience of Christ. At that time, you will have the out-resurrection as the top enjoyment. Therefore, the enjoyment is Christ, the experience is Christ, the goal is Christ, and the prize is Christ. Christ is the enjoyment within us, and Christ is the goal set before us. We need to pursue toward the goal so that we may gain the prize.

To pursue Christ in this way we need to be aggressive and to exercise ourselves very much. No lazy person can be a persecutor of Christ. Every persecutor of Christ has a strong character. I say again that we all must pursue Christ in a persecuting way. We need to pray, "Lord Jesus, I intend to persecute You. All day long I shall be Your persecutor. I will compel You to be for me and to be my experience." Have you ever prayed in this way? We need to pray like this, telling the Lord that we shall persecute Him until He becomes our experience. If we do this, eventually we shall arrive at the goal and receive the prize.

THE ABOVE CALLING

The prize spoken of in Philippians 3:14 is the prize of God's above calling (Gk.). God is in the heavens calling us. Not only has He called us, but He continues to call us.

Furthermore, as we run the race and pursue toward the goal, the angels are cheering us on. What an impressive picture this is!

If we mean business with the Lord, we must be a persecutor of Christ. All the lovers of Jesus should be His persecutors. We should say, "Lord Jesus, because I love You, I shall persecute You until I persuade You to be for me." The Lord Jesus appreciates this. For example, any husband would like his wife to be such a loving persecutor. Suppose a wife would say to her husband, "I shall persecute you until you stay home with me so that I can love you. l love you, and I don't want to lose your presence. You must stay home to enjoy my love." Surely any husband would appreciate such a wife. This is the best way to love the Lord and to seek Him. We should say, "Lord, even if You want to go, I will not let You go. You must stay with me." The seeker in Song of Songs persecuted the Lord in this way. Even if He had begged her to let Him go, she would have refused. May we all persecute the Lord in this way!

THINKING ONE THING

Verse 15 says, "Let us therefore, as many as are full grown, think this: and if anything otherwise ye think, God shall reveal also this unto you" (Gk.). We should not think other things, but just think this one thing. This one thing is to experience Christ. Regardless of what stage of life we are in, we all should think this one thing, that is, to pursue Christ to the uttermost.

WALKING BY THE SAME RULE

Verse 16 continues, "Only this: whereto we have attained, let us walk by the same rule" (Gk.). Even those who are young and not yet full grown should walk by the same rule. Some may think that Paul here is very domineering and speaks like a dictator, even telling the saints what to think. He says that whether they are young or old, experienced or inexperienced, they need to walk by the same rule. This verse should be read in the light of chapter two, verse 2, which says, "Make my joy full, that ye think the same thing, having the same love, one in soul, thinking the one thing" (Gk.). Furthermore, in Philippians 4:2 Paul says, "I beseech Euodias, and beseech Syntyche, to think the same thing in the Lord" (Gk.). The trouble among today's Christians is that nearly everyone thinks a different thing. It is difficult to find one great preacher who works together with another. On the contrary, each one has his own empire and thinks and speaks his own thing. This is the reason that there is nothing but division and confusion in Christianity today. We must not repeat the history of Christianity. The way to be kept from such a sad repetition is to think the one thing. The one thing that we are to think is revealed in Philippians 3:7-15: It is Christ as our experience, enjoyment, goal, and prize.

NEITHER IMPOSING NOR OPPOSING

When some hear that we should think the one thing, they may ask about things such as foot-washing or speaking in tongues. If you want to practice foot-washing or tongues-speaking, you should be free to do so. But do not impose these practices on others. Regarding matters like this, we should not either impose or oppose, because either imposing or opposing will cause difficulty.

In 1963 some from a Pentecostal group and some from a group with a Brethren background proposed that we come together in Los Angeles to practice the church life in oneness. I told them that it is wonderful for Christians from different groups to come together to practice the church life, but that in order to have the church life we all had to drop our differences. I pointed out that if we want to have the Body spoken of in Romans 12, we must learn the lessons in Romans 14. Without Romans 14 it is impossible to have Romans 12. Furthermore, I told them that Christians have been divided and still are divided over various practices. Thus, if we want to have the oneness in the proper church life, we must drop all the differences. Those from each group said they were happy with this and promised to drop the differences. However, in just a few weeks problems developed over the matters of speaking in tongues and playing a tambourine in the meetings. Those from the group with the

Brethren background simply could not tolerate these things. Neither those who favored speaking in tongues and playing the tambourine nor those who opposed these practices would listen to any word about not insisting on their way. Eventually that meeting had to be disbanded.

We should not oppose anything unless it involves idolatry or fornication. Some have asked me about the so-called holy rolling. I said, "If someone is so repentant over his sins that he wants to roll on the floor, that is all right. We should not oppose it. But if someone insists upon this or imposes it upon others, he is divisive. We bear with anything or go along with any practice as long as it is not sinful or a cause of division."

In 1966 we began to practice pray-reading, and in 1968, the calling on the name of the Lord. I can testify that I never insisted upon these practices. However, in a certain place messages were repeatedly given opposing pray-reading and calling on the name of the Lord. As Christians, we need to see that we are not here for a particular practice or for a certain way. Rather, we are for one thing—to pursue after Christ. We all need to think this one thing and to walk by this same rule. If someone is so happy in a meeting that he jumps up and down, I would not oppose him. However, if someone seeks to impose this practice on others, insisting that all the saints or all the churches engage in it, I would not agree with it, because we are not for jumping, but for pursuing after Christ. We do not impose anything nor do we oppose anything. Instead, we are simply pursuing the all-inclusive Christ. We are not here for any way or practice; we are here only to pursue the Lord and to be conformed to His death.

Whatever we do must be done by being conformed to the death of Christ. If we do everything in this way, there will be no problems, and we shall surely think the one thing. Christ must be our experience, goal, and prize. Christ is everything. In the Lord's recovery there is nothing but Christ. This is the only way for us to take in the Lord's recovery.

Although the situation in Philippi was very good, unlike the situation in Corinth, there was still a problem because the saints there were not all thinking the same thing. Thus,

ONE THING TO DO

Paul besought Euodias and Syntyche, two of his co-workers in the gospel, to think the same thing. It is possible that one of the sisters was in favor of Judaism. Whether or not this was so, the fact remains that they were not thinking the one thing. According to the first chapter of Philippians, there was envy and rivalry even in the preaching of the gospel (vv. 15-16). Surely this was an indication that some were not thinking the one thing. This is the reason that in chapter two Paul asked the saints in Philippi to make his joy full. If there was any fellowship in spirit, any comfort of love, any compassion and mercy, they were to make Paul's joy full. He wanted them to make his joy full by thinking the same thing, having the same love, and being one in soul.

We all need to learn to think the one thing, that is, to be occupied with pursuing Christ. We should not be concerned about foot-washing, head covering, speaking in tongues, or any other such matters. Let us leave these things alone and think about the experience and enjoyment of Christ. We need to pray, "Lord, teach me how to persecute You. I don't care for so many other things. I only care to pursue You." Do not be troubled by things such as the playing of a tambourine in the meetings. Playing a tambourine is not our goal, prize, or enjoyment. Our enjoyment, experience, goal, and prize are Christ. If others want to play the tambourine, I shall not oppose it. After they play the tambourine for a certain period of time, there will eventually be an opportunity for me to share Christ with them. This illustrates the fact that we must all learn that for us there is simply one thing: Christ as our experience, enjoyment, goal, and prize. We do not insist on anything, and we do not oppose anything. If we take this way, we shall maintain a good spirit in the churches for the experience and enjoyment of Christ.

We need to honor Christ and allow Him to do everything. Do not persecute Christ regarding things such as speaking in tongues, foot-washing, or playing the tambourine. Instead, persecute Him until He becomes your experience. We need to say, "Lord, it is not up to me whether or not Your people speak in tongues. Lord, I persecute You so that You will be my experience. Lord, when the opportunity comes in the meeting, I would like to share with Your saints something concerning my experience of You." This is the only thing we need to do. Let us all do the same thing and think the one thing. Do not have any other consideration, and do not be bothered by all the different practices. There is only one thing for us to do: pursue Christ and let Him become our experience, enjoyment, goal, and prize.

Chapter Twenty-One

DYING TO LIVE

According to the Bible, death and resurrection are vital both to our Christian life and to God's economy. Apart from death and resurrection, it is impossible for God to accomplish His purpose. Throughout God's creation we see the principle of death and resurrection. For example, if a grain of wheat falls into the earth and dies, it will produce many grains. In John 12:24 the Lord Jesus said, "Truly, truly, I say to you, unless a grain of wheat falls into the ground and dies, it abides alone; but if it dies, it bears much fruit." For a single grain to die and bear much fruit means that it is multiplied into many other grains. Here we see death and resurrection. We also see death and resurrection illustrated in the hatching of a chicken out from an egg. When the shell is broken, the life within it is released, and a baby chicken comes out. Furthermore, the process of death and resurrection is illustrated by the metabolism that takes place in our body. In metabolism something is always dying, and something else is rising up in resurrection. Hence, metabolism is actually a process of death and resurrection. Within us something is always dying so that we may live. Because this matter of death and resurrection is so important to our Christian life, I am burdened to give still another message on the subject of dying to live, a message that will help us see how to be conformed to the death of Christ.

Although we may recognize the need to die, we may not know how to die. Recently, a number of saints have testified that although they have tried to die, they have not been successful in doing so. Not only is it difficult to die; it is even difficult to point out the way to die. I have been in the process of dying for more than fifty years, and I am still learning how to do it. Although it is very difficult to explain what is the way to die, in this message I shall try my best to present the way to you.

GOD WANTING US TO DIE

Regarding this matter, the first thing we Christians need to realize is that God wants us to die. Some Christians hold the mistaken concept that God wants us to die because we are sinful. They may say, "I don't like my sinful old man. Because he is so evil, he must die." Before we were saved, we loved ourselves a great deal and appreciated ourselves very much. But once our being was exposed to the light, we began to hate ourselves. The more light we receive from the Lord, the more we are exposed; and the more we are exposed, the more we hate our ugly self. Thus, many Christians think that we must die because we are so evil, sinful, and ugly. This concept, however, is not accurate. The Lord Jesus had to die, not only on the cross, but also daily during His life on earth, and He certainly was not sinful. On the contrary, He was altogether right and lovable in the eyes of God. There was nothing evil about Him. Nevertheless, even such a pure, perfect, lovable, and sinless Person had to die. When He came forth to minister, the first thing He did was to present Himself to John the Baptist to be buried. Even the Lord Jesus had to die.

If we would know how to die, we need to see clearly that the reason we must die is not because we are sinful, but simply because we are human. Since you are a human being, God wants you to die. This has nothing to do with being evil. In fact, the better you are, the more you need to die. Therefore, we need to have a change of concept about the necessity of dying. We must die because God's economy requires us to die. Even the Lord Jesus, the holy, perfect, sinless, lovable One, had to die. Then what about us? We must die also, not because we are evil, but because we are human. Do not think that you must die because you hate others. No, you must die because you love others so much. The more loving we are, the more we need to die. God's economy requires this.

DYING TO LIVE OUT GOD

The second point concerning the way to die is that God wants us to live out not our human life, but the divine life. In other words He does not want us to live out ourselves; He wants us to live out Him. In order to live out God, we need to die.

The only part of our being that is useful to God is our will. God wants us to exercise our will to choose Him to be our life. Again, I say, He does not want us to live out ourselves. The more we live out ourselves, the more we offend God and rebel against Him. God's economy is to have Himself lived out by us. However, we are doing our best to live out ourselves. This is rebellion. Some say, "I shall live out myself by loving others and by helping them." But God says, "Your loving of others and your helping them are rebellion against Me. I don't want you to love others or to help them. I want you to take Me as your life and to live Me out as your living. If you fail to do this, you are against My economy, and that is rebellion." How important it is for us all to see that God's economy is that we must die in order to live out God!

WHAT IS MOST PLEASING TO THE LORD

The next thing we need to see about how to die is that nothing pleases God as much as our living by Him. This is the most pleasant thing to the Lord. If we take Him as our life and live Him out, His heart is touched, and He is joyful. Marriage is an illustration of this. Nothing touches a husband's heart more than having his wife live according to him. How happy a husband is whenever his wife lives according to him! Likewise, the Lord is very pleased when we live by Him.

In 1933 I was invited to a province in southern China where we were served rice to eat three times a day. As a northerner, I was accustomed to eating wheat instead of rice. Realizing that I was exhausted by the strenuous work of ministering in several meetings a day, some sisters decided to prepare some wheat bread for me. Although, they made this bread out of love, it tasted so bad that I could not eat it. I did not say a word to them, but inwardly I thought that I would rather eat their rice. This illustrates the fact that even though we may do something for others in a loving way, what we do may be not at all pleasing to them because it is done according to ourselves. If a wife loves her husband in this way, she will kill him with her love. What is most pleasing to others is that we live according to them. In like manner, the most pleasing thing to God is that we live by Him in order to live Him out.

ALREADY DEAD

We have seen that God wants us to die, that He wants us to live Him out, and that the most pleasing thing to Him is that we not only live for Him, but live by Him. Now we come to the fourth point concerning how to die. This point is that there is no need for us to die because we have died already. Romans 6:3 says, "Or are you ignorant that as many as have been baptized into Christ Jesus have been baptized into His death?" According to this verse, we should not be ignorant of the fact that we have already been baptized into Christ's death. This indicates that we are already dead. Since we are dead, why should we try to die? How foolish! Are you ignorant of the fact that you have already been baptized into Christ's death? No, we are not ignorant. We know that we have been baptized into Christ's death.

Furthermore, Romans 6:4 says, "We have been buried therefore with Him through baptism into death." This verse does not say that we shall be buried; it says that we have been buried. Have you been buried? Then why are you still trying to die? How can a buried person die? How ridiculous! The Bible says that we have been buried, and we must believe it.

Notice that Romans 6:4 says that we have been buried with Him through baptism into death. Ordinarily, death comes first and then burial. But here the sequence is burial first and death second, for we are buried into Christ's death. This indicates that before we were buried, we were living. Thus, the way to die is by being buried into Christ's death. This is the biblical way. Hallelujah, we have been buried! There is no need for us to be buried because we have been buried into death already.

CHRIST AND HIS DEATH

According to Romans 6:3, to be baptized into Christ is equal to being baptized into His death. Furthermore, verse 4 says that we have been buried with Christ through baptism into death. Thus, in this portion of the Word, death equals Christ and Christ, death. Whenever I experience the death of Christ to a rich degree, I realize that the Lord Himself is death to me.

If we all remain in the death of Christ, there will be no problems. The reason a husband has difficulties with his wife is that he comes out of the death of Christ. Whenever we come out of the death of Christ, we cause trouble. If everyone in the church life remains in the death of Christ, all the problems will disappear.

Consider both Romans 6 and your experience. The Bible reveals the wonderful all-inclusive and all-accomplishing death of Christ. We all have been baptized into such a death. This is a fact. As many as have been baptized into Christ have been baptized, buried, into His death. In a very real sense, we Christians need to remain in the death of Christ.

WALKING IN NEWNESS OF LIFE

The whole of Romans 6:4 says, "We have been buried therefore with Him through baptism into death that as Christ was raised from among the dead through the glory of the Father, even so we also should walk in newness of life." The Greek word translated "that" here can be rendered "in order that," pointing to a result, an issue. If we are not buried into Christ's death, we cannot have the result spoken of in this verse. We have been buried into death in order that we may walk in newness of life. The reference to Christ's being raised from among the dead through the glory of the Father indicates a glorious resurrection. As Christ was raised from among the dead in a glorious resurrection, even so we also should walk in newness of life.

However, many do not experience the death of Christ; yet

they endeavor to walk in newness of life. You were the one buried into death. The one who has been resurrected to walk in newness of life is not the original you, the one who was buried; it is Christ with you. We Christians are too natural. Our thinking and our understanding are so natural. We even understand the Bible according to our natural mentality. Because we are still governed by our natural concepts, we may say, "The Bible tells us that we should walk in newness of life. Therefore, let us walk in newness of life." But this is not possible if we have not been buried and if we do not remain in death. If we come out of death, how can we walk in newness of life? It is impossible.

DEATH AND RESURRECTION RELATED TO CHRIST

These verses in Romans 6 also indicate that death and resurrection are related to Christ. Verse 3 says that we have been baptized into Christ and that we have been baptized into His death. This indicates that we cannot be baptized into death apart from Christ. We must be baptized into Christ that we may be baptized into His death. Moreover, verse 4 says that we have been buried with Him. Concerning the matter of death, we cannot be apart from Him. This is also true of resurrection.

This may be difficult to understand, but it is easy to experience. For example, we all breathe constantly. Although I would find it hard to write an article about what breathing is, I nonetheless know how to breathe. When I was an infant, I could breathe without having any knowledge of what breathing was. Likewise, it is easy to experience Christ, but very difficult to explain what we are experiencing. According to my experience, I have been baptized into Christ and into His death. As long as I remain in Him, I remain in death. When I am in Christ, I am in death. The issue, the effect, of this is that I walk in newness of life. Actually, however, it is not I who walk in newness of life; it is Christ. This is proved by Galatians 2:20: "I am crucified with Christ: nevertheless I live; yet not I, but Christ liveth in me." In the light of this verse, we can say that it is Christ and not we who walk in newness of life. We know this by our experience.

THE THRESHOLD OF RESURRECTION

When we remain in the death of Christ, it is not the end; it is the threshold of resurrection. Whenever I remain in the death of Christ, this death brings me into resurrection, and Christ rises up with me. The problem is that we do not remain in the death of Christ. If we do not stay in His death, Christ cannot rise up in us. Resurrection requires the ground of death. Obviously, Christ could not have been resurrected if He had not died. But because He died, He could be resurrected. The principle is the same with us today. The principle of life is that where there is death, there is resurrection.

After considering all these points, we should no longer try to die. Instead, we should cease from all our striving. The first stanza of a hymn expresses this very well:

> Buried with Christ and raised with Him too;
> What is there left for me to do?
> Simply to cease from struggling and strife,
> Simply to walk in newness of life.
> Glory be to God!

If we try anything, we should try doing what this hymn suggests. We have been buried, and Christ is resurrected with us. Day after day, we need to be reminded that we have already been buried and that our position is in death. For us to remain in death is to be like a seed remaining in the earth. Eventually, the life within the seed will rise up. Likewise, when we remain in His death, Christ who is the life within us will rise up.

We are not stones, but grains of wheat. The difference between a stone and a grain of wheat is that the grain of wheat has life in it. When the grain is sown into the soil and remains there, sooner or later the life within the grain will rise up. Likewise, Christ as the life in us will rise up if we stay in His death.

CHRIST BEING THE POWER OF RESURRECTION

If we would know how to die, we must also see that we have a powerful life within us and that this life is Christ.

Second Corinthians 13:3 says, "Since ye seek a proof of Christ speaking in me, which to you-ward is not weak, but is mighty in you." Christ is not weak in us; He is powerful. He is the powerful One. This powerful One is actually the power of resurrection spoken of in Philippians 3:10. Christ Himself is the power of His resurrection. If you take away Christ, resurrection has no power. Hallelujah, today this power of life is in us!

According to Philippians 3:10 and 11, we firstly have the power of resurrection, secondly the conformity to Christ's death, and thirdly the attaining unto the out-resurrection. Thus, the sequence is resurrection, death, resurrection. In our experience, which comes first, death or resurrection? We have already pointed out that death is the threshold of resurrection. Therefore, death must be first. But in these verses resurrection comes before death. Romans 6 says that we are baptized into Christ's death and indicates that the power of resurrection follows death. In Philippians 3 death is implied by the fact that Paul counted all things loss. Paul's counting all things loss was actually his experience of remaining in the death of Christ. Because he remained in death, the power of Christ's resurrection could rise up in him. This is the way to know the power of resurrection.

The way to know the life power in a grain of wheat is to put that grain into the soil and keep it there. Likewise, in order to know Christ as the power of resurrection life within us, we need to remain in Christ's death. As we remain in His death, the power of life will rise up. When the power of life rises up, it will bring us into deeper death. This deeper death is the conformity to Christ's death.

The day we were baptized we were merely put into Christ's death; we were not yet conformed to it. For example, when sisters bake a cake, they put the dough into a mold. But after the dough is put into the mold, it is pressed and processed until it conforms to the mold. Thus, to put the dough into the mold is one thing, and to conform it to the mold is another. When we were baptized, we were put into the death of Christ, but we were not molded to the form of His death. When we are willing to remain in His death, the power of resurrection will rise up within us and bring us deeper and deeper into death. This is not being baptized into His death, but being conformed to His death. We need to say, "Lord, how I thank You for Your wonderful death. To stay here is not a suffering. How sweet and pleasant it is to remain in Your death! When someone gives me a difficult time, I would like to remain in this death and sing hymns of praise unto You." If we remain in Christ's death in such a way, we shall have resurrection. The more resurrection we have, the more death we shall experience. Eventually, the out-resurrection, the outstanding resurrection, will be ours.

REMAINING IN THE DEATH OF CHRIST

Many brothers and sisters have been baptized into Christ's death, but they do not remain in death. I can tell by the expression on their faces that they have come out of death, for it is obvious that they are not at rest. Everyone who remains in death is at rest. If we remain in death, we shall be able to say, "I don't have problems with anyone. I am simply resting here. Whether others appreciate me or rebuke me, I am not disturbed. Rather I am at rest." The reason there is conflict between a husband and wife is that they so often come out of death. By leaving death, they lose their rest. Some brothers and sisters may come all the way out of death, whereas others may have one foot in death and one foot outside death. When they go back into death, they are at rest, but when they come out, they lose their rest. Some may remain in death, but instead of lying down in it, they stand up and try to get out. Still others may lie down in death; however, they are only partly at rest because as they lie there, they are desiring to leave death. Only those who fully rest in death actually remain in Christ's death. These can say, "Praise the Lord that I have been baptized into His death. I am content to stay here."

THE CYCLE OF DEATH AND RESURRECTION

Those who remain in death know the power of resurrection. As they lie restfully in death, they have the experience of Philippians 3:10. They know Christ, the power of His resurrection, and the fellowship of His sufferings. They are also conformed to Christ's death like dough conformed to a mold.

From now on, we should not only be in Christ's death, but also be conformed to His death. The more we are conformed to His death, the more we know the power of His resurrection; and the more we know the power of His resurrection, the more we are conformed to His death. It is in this way that we pass through the process of resurrection that leads to the out-resurrection. The more death there is, the more resurrection; and the more resurrection, the more death. This is a cycle that moves like a wheel. This is the Christian life and also the Christian walk. We live and walk by this cycle.

This cycle begins, not with resurrection, but with death. Are you ignorant of the fact that as many of us as have been baptized into Christ have been baptized into His death? Being baptized into the death of Christ is the beginning of the cycle. Through this experience of death, resurrection power rises up within us to bring us into deeper death. After we enter deeper into death, more resurrection power rises up. In this way the cycle continues from death to resurrection and from resurrection to death. Eventually, we shall arrive at the outstanding resurrection. That will be the time of our maturity, the time when we are ready for rapture and the redemption of our body. The redemption of the body is the last step of resurrection. When our physical body enters into resurrection, it will be transfigured. That will be the full maturity of our Christian life.

The Christian life is a matter of dying to live. We die so that we may live. If there is no death, there can be no life, no resurrection. The more death we have, the more resurrection we experience; and the more resurrection we have, the more death we experience. This is the cycle that is gradually bringing us to maturity until we arrive at the outstanding resurrection. This is the Christian life.

CHAPTER TWENTY-TWO

COOPERATING WITH THE SPIRIT

In this message we come to our need to cooperate with the Spirit. As we pointed out in the last message, we must die in order to live. This is very mysterious. The proper and genuine Christian life is a life of dying, yet living. For example, if you do not allow a seed to die by sowing it into the ground, it cannot live. But if it falls into the ground and dies, it will grow. Hence, it grows by dying. Without dying, the life in the seed cannot grow. The life is there, but it is not living. In order for the life in the seed to be living, the seed must die. How mysterious this is! Although it is a mystery, this principle operates throughout the universe, in the plant life, in the animal life, in the human life, and even in the divine life. God became a man to die so that He might live out God. The Lord Jesus said, "Unless a grain of wheat falls into the ground and dies, it abides alone; but if it dies, it bears much fruit" (John 12:24). If a grain of wheat does not fall into the ground and die, there will be no growing, no living. But if it dies, it will produce many grains. Here we see the principle of life growing through death. Where death is, there life is growing. This principle applies not only to the plant and animal life, but also to the human life and even the divine life.

THE PILOT AND THE CO-PILOT

In the process of dying, we need to cooperate with the Spirit. On many airplanes there are a pilot and a co-pilot. The co-pilot must cooperate with the pilot. As we are dying, we should not operate, but cooperate. It is a terrible thing for us to operate, to try to do something, as we are dying. However, a brother may pray, "Lord, my wife is giving me a difficult time. I must overcome this problem." If you do this, you are wrong, because you are operating instead of cooperating. The word "cooperate" implies that there is someone better than you who is operating. For example, the pilot is better than the co-pilot, for he is first and the co-pilot is second. Sorry to say, most of the time you pilot your own life. The result is misery. The reason your family life is miserable is that you are the pilot instead of the co-pilot. Our pilot is Christ as the wonderful life-giving Spirit. Although we have Him as the Pilot within us, we often do not honor Him, respect Him, or care for Him. Instead, we prefer to be the pilot.

Some Christians may think that as long as Christ is the Pilot, everything is fine. No, everything is not necessarily fine. Although Christ is the Pilot, you need to be the co-pilot. Our practice is either to be the pilot or to be nothing. Both are wrong. Many Christians realize the truth of Galatians 2:20, that they have been crucified with Christ, that they live no longer, and that Christ lives in them. This, however, is just half of the verse. This verse also speaks of "the life which I now live in the flesh." Many Christians either pilot their own life or neglect everything. However, we should do neither of these and avoid both extremes. Our Pilot needs us to be the co-pilot.

NOT A MATTER OF SELF-CRUCIFIXION

Many years ago I read some books which said that we need to crucify ourselves. But these messages were not accurate, for they taught us that we had to crucify ourselves in order to be crucified with Christ. Some years later, Brother Nee pointed out that this teaching was absolutely wrong. No one can commit suicide by crucifixion. It is possible for a person to commit suicide by any number of ways, but not by crucifixion. Everyone who is crucified is helped in this matter by others. Not even the Lord Jesus could put Himself on the cross; rather, the soldiers nailed Him to the cross. Thus, it is definitely not logical to say that we can crucify ourselves. Although we cannot crucify ourselves, we nonetheless thank the Lord that we have been crucified.

At this point, some may ask about Galatians 5:24. This

verse says, "And they that are Christ's have crucified the flesh with the affections and lusts." Notice that this verse does not say that we have crucified ourselves. It says that we have crucified the flesh. Certainly we can crucify the flesh with its passions and lusts. In the Bible the flesh signifies the evil aspect of the body. We all need to crucify our flesh with its passions and lusts. But this does not mean that we are to crucify ourselves.

Another important verse in this regard is Romans 8:13: "For if you live according to flesh, you are about to die; but if by the Spirit you put to death the practices of the body, you will live." This verse indicates that we are to put to death, not only the flesh with its lusts, but also the practices of the body, whether they are good or evil. If we put to death the practices of the body, we shall live. Therefore, we must crucify our flesh and put to death the practices of our body.

Furthermore, in Matthew 16:24 the Lord Jesus said, "If anyone desires to come after Me, let him deny himself, and take up his cross, and follow Me." In addition to crucifying our flesh and putting to death the practices of our body, we need to deny ourselves. We must do these things ourselves. No one else can do them for us. The way to deal with the flesh with its passions is to crucify it, the way to deal with the practices of the body is to put them to death, and the way to deal with the self is to deny it.

OUR DUAL STATUS

We have spoken of our need to cooperate with the Spirit. The reason we need to cooperate with the Spirit is that, as saved people, we have a dual status. Before we were saved, we had just one status. But after we were saved, another life, or another Person, came into us. The One who came into us is Christ as the life-giving Spirit. It is a fact, not a superstition or a doctrine, that another Person, Jesus Christ Himself as the life-giving Spirit, has come into our being. When He came into us, He came not into our mind nor into our flesh, but into our spirit. Thus, at the time we were saved, the life-giving Spirit was added to our spirit. This addition of the Triune God into us caused our spirit to be regenerated.

Now as regenerated ones, we have a dual status. Regarding the first aspect of this dual status, we are dying; and regarding the second aspect, in our regenerated spirit where Christ is, we are living. Not one verse in the Bible says that we must crucify our spirit, put our spirit to death, or deny our spirit. But, as we have already pointed out, there are verses telling us that our flesh with its passions must be crucified, that the practices of our body must be put to death, and that the self must be denied. In this we see our dual status: one status with the flesh, the body, and the self; and another status with the spirit indwelt by the life-giving Spirit.

We have seen that the first status comprises the flesh, the practices of the body, and the self. In this status are we living or dying? We are dying. But as we die in the first status, we need to cooperate with the second. Therefore, in the first status we are dying, but in the second status we are cooperating with the Spirit. Hallelujah for our dual status! The first status is fully qualified for death, and the second is qualified for cooperation. In our second status, that is, in our spirit, we have a wonderful Pilot who manages our life. Nevertheless, He needs us to be His co-pilots. As His co-pilots who are dying in the first status, we need to cooperate with the Spirit in our second status.

DYING AND LIVING

The more we die, the more living we become. If we all die, then we shall be very living in the meetings. When what we are according to our first status is kept in the tomb, what we are according to our second status, the spirit, rises up. As we are dying, we live by cooperating with the life-giving Spirit. On the negative side we need to do three things: crucify the flesh, put to death the practices of the body, and deny the self. It is not good enough to be tired of these things; we need to die to them. How wonderful it is to die to the flesh, to the practices of the body, and to the self! We need to cooperate with the life-giving Spirit to deal with these three things on the negative side. Whenever the flesh expresses itself, perhaps in anger, we need to cooperate with the Spirit to crucify it.

This is not mere doctrine, but something we have learned through our experience. I did not learn this from a book, but from my experience. For years I tried various ways to deal with these things, but none of them worked. In particular, I followed the teaching about reckoning ourselves dead. However, although I tried my best to reckon myself dead, it did not work. In fact, the more I reckoned myself dead, the more alive I was.

Eventually, by experience I learned that as we are dying, we need to cooperate with the Spirit. The more we die in our first status, the more living we become in the second status. This means that our spirit rises up. As our spirit rises up, we need to cooperate with the Spirit in us to crucify the flesh, to put to death the practices of the body, and to deny the self. We need to pray, "Lord, I know that the secret of the spiritual life is not firstly to live, but to die that I may live. Lord, I pray that You will help me to die." You need not bear the responsibility for living. Simply take care of dying. If you take care of dying to live, the Lord will take the responsibility of living.

To die actually means to be conformed to Christ's death. The Christian life is a life of dying. In our Christian life there is a mold, and that mold is the death of Christ. Like dough that is pressed into a mold, we need to be pressed into the mold of Christ's death until we are conformed to it. Do not try to live. Instead, you simply need to die. Wherever we are, especially at home, we need to die. When the young people get married, they should not get married to live, but to die. All the problems in married life come from the fact that we are still living. But whenever we die, we are rescued and are at peace. We are happy when we die, but in misery when we try to live.

PUTTING TO DEATH THE GOOD PRACTICES

When we die, Christ lives in us, rising up not simply by Himself, but with our spirit. We need to cooperate with His rising up within us. Therefore, we die in our first status and cooperate with Him in our second status. When the Spirit as the Pilot is about to crucify our flesh, we, the co-pilots, must cooperate. If the Spirit tells us to crucify the flesh, we need to be willing to do so. If we do this, the Spirit will be happy. Then the Spirit will proceed to put to death all the practices of the body, including such things as our humility, love, and good intentions. Do not reason with the Spirit by saying that such practices of the body are good. Because we are not willing to put to death such practices, we bargain with the Spirit and say, "These are very good practices. For example, this is my practice of humility and that is my practice of helping others." Nevertheless, the Lord will tell us to put these practices to death. However, not many of us are willing to do this.

I have struggled with the Lord regarding this for years. Sometimes there was no struggle because I persisted in thinking that my love, humility, helpfulness, and work for the Lord were good. Yes, they may have been good, but they were natural. It took years for me to learn this. How often I offended the Lord and even rebelled against Him by being good! Eventually, I repented and prayed, "Lord, forgive me. not only of my sins, but also of my goodness. Lord, forgive me for doing so many good things for You." Have you ever made such a confession? In confessing, we may think that we need to confess only evil things, but not good things. Have you ever made a confession concerning your love or work for the Lord? Have you ever confessed the good things you have done to help the saints? Under the Lord's mercy, I have confessed my good works as much as my sins. Romans 8:13 says that by the Spirit we must put to death the practices of the body. This includes both good and evil practices. To do something by our body means to do it by the self. We must repent of everything we have done in ourselves and then put these things to death.

DENYING THE SELF

Along with crucifying the flesh and putting to death the practices of the body, we need to deny the self. This is a very subjective matter. According to Matthew 16:23 and 24, the self is the personification of Satan. The inward reality of the self is Satan. Peter made a good proposal to the Lord, but the Lord saw through the outward self and perceived that Satan was hiding there. Thus, the Lord exposed Satan by saying to Peter, "Get behind Me, Satan!" Immediately after saying this, the Lord spoke about denying the self, the very self that is the embodiment of Satan. Because Satan himself is in our self, we must deny it.

In ourselves we are not able to deal with the flesh, the practices of the body, or the satanic self. For years, we have tried to be the pilot, but we have failed. No longer should we try to be the pilot. We have a wonderful Pilot, the life-giving Spirit, in us; we just need to cooperate with Him.

CONTACTING THE LORD

Now we come to the most crucial point in this message: It is absolutely necessary for us to contact the Lord. Day by day and hour by hour, we need to contact the Lord. We need to pray, watch, and maintain good fellowship with Him. This is what it means to cooperate. The initial step in cooperating with the Spirit is to contact the Lord continually. As we contact Him, we must be ready all the time to go along with the leading of the indwelling Spirit. Do not argue or reason with Him, but do whatever He leads you to do. You may not have the strength to do it, but if you contact the Lord and are willing to go along with the Spirit, He will strengthen you. This will make it easy for you to obey Him. In this way your obedience will become your cooperation with the Spirit.

Throughout the centuries, thousands of the lovers of Jesus have contacted Him and lived in His presence, although they did not have as much light or knowledge as we do. But because they loved the Lord so much, they were willing and happy to obey the Spirit within them. Thus, they experienced what we have been talking about in this message. They did not have the knowledge, but they did have the experience. Through their willingness to go along with the indwelling Spirit, they experienced the crucifixion of the flesh, the putting to death of the practices of the body, and the denial of the self. This is the way to be conformed to Christ's death.

THE TOP RESURRECTION BEING OUR PORTION

Here, in the conformity to the death of Christ, the top resurrection is our portion. When we die, Christ's resurrection power rises up to lift us into the top resurrection. This makes the outstanding resurrection our experience today. I have not learned this from books; I have learned it from my experience. Through experience I have discovered that by being conformed to the mold of the death of Christ, resurrection power rises up to bring us into the outstanding resurrection the extraordinary resurrection, as our daily portion. In this way, we live a crucified yet resurrected life. By this death and resurrection we experience Christ, and the riches of Christ become our portion. In this way we experience Christ through death and resurrection and enjoy Him as our portion in our daily life.

Chapter Twenty-Three

IN THE EMPOWERING ONE

Regarding the experience of Christ, the book of Philippians is the most wonderful Epistle in the New Testament. Philippians 1:20 indicates that in any situation Christ can be magnified in us. In the next verse Paul says, "For to me to live is Christ." Chapter two takes us deeper into the experience of Christ. Verses 12 and 13 of this chapter reveal that we need to obey the inner working of God. God is working in us both the willing and the working for His good pleasure (v. 13, Gk.), but we still need to work out our own salvation daily. Day by day, we need to be saved, rescued, and delivered. We work out such a daily salvation by obeying God's inner working. In chapter three Paul proceeds to tell us that we need the excellency of the knowledge of Christ Jesus the Lord (v. 8). This means that we need the excellency in knowing Christ. On account of this excellency, we should count everything loss. Furthermore, we should suffer the loss of all things and count them dung in order to gain Christ and to be found in Him. Paul was a person absolutely in Christ. For this reason, in 2 Corinthians 12:2 he refers to himself as "a man in Christ." As a man in Christ, his desire was to be found always in Christ. Being found in Christ, he did not have his own righteousness, but the righteousness that was God Himself lived out of him. Because he lived in this condition, he could know Christ, the power of His resurrection, and the fellowship of His suffering. All this enabled him to be conformed to the death of Christ so that, by any means, he might arrive at the out-resurrection from among the dead.

BEING IN CHRIST

In Philippians 4 Paul says that he had learned the secret

both to abound and to suffer need (v. 12, Gk.). In everything and in all things he had learned the secret. Paul can declare, "I can do all things in the One who empowers me" (v. 13, Gk.). Thus, at the end of the book of Philippians, we find a man who could do everything in Christ.

The secret of doing all things is to be in Christ. John 15:5 affords a contrast to this. In this verse the Lord says, "Apart from Me you can do nothing." Therefore, Philippians 4:13 says that we can do all things in Him, and John 15:5 says that apart from Him we can do nothing. We all need to learn to say, "Apart from Him I can do nothing, but in Him I can do all things." The secret is to be in Him.

THE SECRET OF BEING IN CHRIST

I am concerned that many of us do not know how to be in Christ. You may say, "Today, we are all in Christ." Yes, doctrinally we are in Him, but experientially we may not be in Him. First Corinthians 1:30 says that of God are we in Christ. Furthermore, Romans 6:3 and Galatians 3:27 say that we have been baptized into Christ. Thus, we have all been put into Christ. However, the Bible also says that after we have been put into Christ, we need to abide, remain, stay, in Him (John 15:4). To be put into Christ is one thing, and to remain in Christ is another. Being put into Christ does not depend upon us; it is a sovereign act of God. How we thank God that we are in Christ! To abide in Christ, however, does not depend on God; it depends on us. Now that God has put us into Christ, we need to abide in Him. But after we have been put into Christ, we may stay there for only a short time and then not remain in Him.

THE SECRET OF ABIDING IN CHRIST

The first secret in this message is that in order to do all things we need to be in Christ; the second secret is that to be in Christ we must abide in Him. For us to be in Him is to abide, remain, stay, in Him. Now we need to learn the secret of how to abide in Him. To be in Him is a secret, to abide in Him is a secret, and to know how to abide in Him is still another secret. Concerning this matter of abiding in

Christ, the New Testament does not leave us in darkness. The same Apostle who wrote about abiding in Christ in his Gospel also spoke about this in his first Epistle. According to 1 John 2:27, the way to abide in Christ is to take care of the anointing, for the anointing teaches us to abide in Him. Therefore, the secret of abiding in Christ is to care for the anointing. We must abide in Him according to the anointing.

I assume that we all know that the anointing is the moving and the working of the all-inclusive Spirit within us. The all-inclusive Spirit is the compound Spirit typified by the compound ointment in Exodus 30:22-33. The compound ointment described there pictures the contents of the all-inclusive Spirit. One of these ingredients pictures the all-inclusive death of Christ, and another portrays the resurrection. This compound Spirit is very active within us; He is moving, operating, working. His moving within us is a kind of teaching, and this teaching is like a sign or indicator. For example, as you drive your car, you see red and green lights, as well as many other road signs. These signs show you when and how to drive. Likewise, the teaching of the compound Spirit within us shows us how to abide in Christ. We abide in Him by the teaching of the inner anointing.

THE SECRET OF CARING FOR THE ANOINTING

We have seen that the secret of doing all things is to be in Him, that the secret of being in Him is to abide, and that the secret of abiding is to take care of the inner anointing. But now we must learn the secret of how to take care of the anointing. Every saved person has the anointing within. But day by day and hour by hour, most do not take care of it. Before I go on, let me give an example of not taking care of the anointing. Suppose the brothers living in a brothers' house are all very natural and talk with one another in a natural way. There is no need for them to exercise their will to talk, for the words simply pour out of their mouths. Early in the morning, one brother may ask another about his roommate. The two begin to talk, and this talk opens the gates of Hades. As these brothers are talking, something within them is saying, "Don't talk." That brief word is the teaching of the anointing, which is nothing less than the living and the working of the indwelling Christ. However, the brothers may keep on talking and thus disobey the anointing.

Although the indwelling Christ is living in us, too often we do not live with Him. He lives His way, but we live our way. When we rise up in the morning, He desires to live His life, but we live our life. This causes a discrepancy, and this discrepancy is abnormal. Normally, Christ should live in us, and we should live according to His living. In this way, we live by Him. This, however, should not be mere doctrine; it must be our daily living. For example, instead of talking in a natural way, we should talk when He talks. He speaks within, and we express His speaking. If He does not talk, then we should not talk either. In this way He talks in our talking. This is one life coming from two persons. We as the first person are the expression of the inner person, who is Christ.

In doctrine we may be very clear about this, but we may not practice it in our daily life. I am not concerned for doctrine, but for your living. In your daily life do you live the life that Christ is living within you? Perhaps as you get up in the morning, you want to talk, but He does not. In such a case there is a discrepancy between your living and His. Normally, your living and His living should be one. But instead of this, in your talking too often there are two persons with two different livings instead of two persons with one living. Therefore, as you are about to talk about a certain brother, the Lord, who does not want to talk, moves within you to give you a certain feeling. You sense something moving within. Nevertheless, many times you do not care for this inner feeling. Thus, although the Lord does not want to talk, you proceed to talk anyway, sometimes gossiping for more than an hour. All this talk is disobedient to God's inner working. When you gossip in this way, you are not obeying the anointing.

The problem here is that in our talking we very often get off the cross. When Christ was on the cross, He was tempted to prove that He was the Son of God by coming down from the cross (Matt. 27:40). Although the Lord did not come down from the cross, we do so very often, even many times in one day. I must confess that this has been my own experience. I am familiar with this illness because I have suffered from it myself for years. Therefore, I can illustrate this according to my experience. Early in the morning, I may talk too much. Unable to eat breakfast in a good way because I am condemned for this, I go to my room and confess to the Lord, saying, "Lord, I confess how natural I am. Please forgive me. I hate my natural man and my talkativeness. Lord, put my tongue on the cross." Every kind of repentance and confession is a killing. After being killed in this way, I am on the cross again. But later in the day some brothers may come to visit me, and again I may find myself talking too much. Although something within tells me to be quiet, I keep talking. It seems that there are no brakes on my spiritual car. Later, I regret my talkativeness and confess to the Lord once again. This time it is difficult even to speak to the Lord, because I feel so ashamed in His presence. Nevertheless, I ask Him to forgive me once again. Through my confession, I get on the cross once again. I believe that this is not only my experience, but also yours.

The problem is that we get off the cross. Yes, it is a fact that we have been crucified with Christ, but are we on the cross right now? The secret of taking care of the inner anointing is to stay on the cross.

THE SECRET OF STAYING ON THE CROSS

This brings us to still another secret, the secret of staying on the cross. Because it is impossible for us to do this ourselves, we must find the secret of doing it. The secret of staying on the cross is that Christ is within us as resurrection power. Remember, Philippians 3:10 speaks of knowing Christ, the power of His resurrection, and the fellowship of His sufferings; it also speaks of being conformed to His death. Being conformed to His death comes after knowing the power of Christ's resurrection. Through the power of resurrection that is within us we are conformed to His death. Although we cannot keep ourselves on the cross, within us there is the power of resurrection, and by this power we can stay on the cross. When we stay on the cross, we are not committing suicide, because we are not actually keeping ourselves there; it is the power of resurrection that keeps us there.

In the foregoing message, we considered Galatians 5:24, which says that those that are Christ's have crucified the flesh with its passions and lusts (Gk.). This crucifixion of the flesh takes place by the Spirit. This is indicated by the fact that the next verse says that if we have life in the Spirit, we should also walk in the Spirit. This indicates the crucifying of the flesh takes place by the Spirit within us. Therefore, we are not actually the ones who crucify it; it is the Spirit as the power of resurrection who does this. In this regard we need to remember Romans 8:13, which says that by the Spirit we put to death the practices of the body. We have the Spirit within us. No matter how weak we may be, He is in us as the source of our experience of crucifixion. We cannot crucify our flesh or put to death the practices of the body, but the Spirit can do it. This is why, as we pointed out in the previous message, we need to cooperate with the indwelling Spirit.

We have also seen that Matthew 16:24 says that we must deny the self. However, not even the denial of the self can be done by ourselves; rather, it is done by the One who lives in us. By Him, it is easy for us to deny the self. But apart from Him it is impossible. Regarding the denial of the self, there is One within us who is always waiting for our cooperation. If we say, "Amen," He will do the work and keep us on the cross.

This experience of the cross is not a suffering, but an enjoyment. We enjoy the gracious working of the indwelling Spirit. Hour after hour and day after day, this indwelling Spirit keeps us on the cross. Therefore, by the Spirit as the power of resurrection, we are being conformed to Christ's death. The result of this is that we arrive at the out-resurrection from among the dead (Phil. 3:11, Gk.). The power of resurrection works to conform us to Christ's death. Then by our being conformed to His death, the out-resurrection becomes our portion. Thus, resurrection gives us the experience of death, which in turn brings us to the out-resurrection. This is the reason that A. B. Simpson could say in one of his hymns,

"'Tis not hard to die with Christ when His risen life we know." Because we have resurrection life within us, it is not difficult to die. In another of his hymns A. B. Simpson says, "Oh! it is so sweet to die with Christ" Because Christ is in us, it is sweet to die with Him. The resurrected One in us is the One who has experienced the crucifixion. Thus, it is not hard for us to die. On the contrary, it is sweet to die with Him because by dying with Him we enjoy Him.

Resurrection brings us into death, and death ushers us into higher resurrection, even the outstanding resurrection. Our natural life, desires, intentions, and tendencies are crucified, not by ourselves, but by the indwelling Spirit. This is the way to take care of the inner anointing. By taking care of the inner anointing, we abide in Him; by abiding in Him, we are in Him; and by being in Him we can do all things.

THE SECRET OF ENJOYING THE INDWELLING SPIRIT

In this message we have seen five secrets: the first is that to do all things we need to be in Him; the second, that to be in Him we need to abide in Him; the third, that to abide in Him we need to take care of the anointing; the fourth, that to take care of the anointing we need to remain on the cross; and the fifth, that in order to stay on the cross we must depend upon the indwelling Spirit. Although we have seen these five secrets, we must still consider a sixth—the secret of how to enjoy the indwelling Spirit. First Thessalonians 5:16 through 18 say, "Rejoice evermore. Pray without ceasing. In everything give thanks: for this is the will of God in Christ Jesus concerning you." Instead of periods after verses 16 and 17, there should be commas. This change of punctuation indicates that rejoicing evermore, praying without ceasing, and giving thanks in everything are the will of God in Christ Jesus concerning us. God has a will regarding us. This will is that we must constantly rejoice, pray, and give thanks. This is the sixth and last secret, the practical secret. Without it, all the other secrets mean nothing.

Because we are so forgetful, we need to practice remembering all these secrets. Therefore, let us go over them again. The first secret is that if we would be able to do all things, we need to be in Christ. The second secret is that to be in Him requires that we abide in Him. The third secret is that to abide in Him we need to take care of the inner anointing. The fourth secret is that in order to take care of the inner anointing we must remain on the cross. We have seen that we in ourselves are not able to stay on the cross; instead, we often come down from the cross. Hence, we need to know the fifth secret: remaining on the cross by means of the indwelling Spirit. But all this is of no avail without the sixth secret, the secret of how to enjoy the indwelling Spirit. This secret is to rejoice always, to pray without ceasing, and to give thanks in everything.

Suppose as I am ministering, a brother stands up and says, "Brother Lee, I don't agree with your speaking. You must stop." At such a time I need to rejoice. To fail to rejoice is to get off the cross. Thus, if a brother rebukes me and tells me to stop speaking, I should say, "Praise the Lord! Hallelujah! How happy I am!" The sisters should also do this when their husbands give them a difficult time. Sisters, instead of being troubled by your husbands, rejoice in the Lord. Whenever we are not rejoicing, we come down from the cross. The indwelling Spirit works with us in our rejoicing.

For years I have encouraged the saints to release the spirit and to exercise the spirit. Now I wish to point out that the best way to release the spirit is to rejoice. To rejoice is not merely to be happy; it is to make a joyful noise. When we are joyful, we rejoice.

In 1 Thessalonians 5 the word "rejoice" is modified by the word "evermore," and the word "pray" by the words "without ceasing." Furthermore, in everything we are to give thanks to God. This means that even if a sister's husband gives her a difficult time, she should praise the Lord. Rejoicing always, praying unceasingly, and giving thanks in everything is the will of God. These three things, which have been ordained by God, are like small screws in a machine. But without these screws, the entire machine cannot operate.

Whenever we fail to give thanks in something, the indwelling Spirit is choked. In 1 Thessalonians 5 the matter of not quenching the Spirit is related to rejoicing evermore, to praying without ceasing, and to giving thanks in all things. If you do not rejoice, you quench the Spirit. If you do not pray or give thanks, you also quench the Spirit. The way to stir up the Spirit is to rejoice always, to pray unceasingly, and to give thanks in everything. The Spirit here is the power of resurrection. Although we have this Spirit within us, the Spirit is often choked because we do not rejoice, pray, or give thanks.

KEEPING CERTAIN LEGALITIES

In order to be healthy, we need to keep four legalities: eating, drinking, breathing, and sleeping. Although Christians often condemn legality, we need to be legal about these things. In so many other things we should not be legal, but when it comes to eating, drinking, breathing, and sleeping, we must be legal. In like manner, rejoicing, praying, and giving thanks in all things are legalities. When some brothers hear this, they may say, "Brother Lee, I cannot thank the Lord for a wife such as mine. You don't know how bad she is. If you had such a wife, you would sympathize with me." However, no matter what kind of wife a brother has, he must rejoice and give thanks in everything. Each of us must do this for himself. Just as we cannot eat, drink, or breathe for others, so we cannot pray, rejoice, or give thanks for others.

An incident that took place in my hometown years ago illustrates this. A certain sister became deceived; she decided to give up eating and pray all day long. We tried our best to convince her to eat, telling her that we were concerned that she would die if she continued to go without eating. However, she still refused to eat. She had a good heart to pray for the church and for the saints. But because she would not eat, she eventually died. We could do many things for her, but we could not eat for her. Eating is a legality that we all must keep for ourselves. In like manner, if you do not pray, rejoice, or give thanks, I do not know what to do for you. The best thing I can do is to ask the Lord to make you willing to pray, to rejoice, and to give thanks.

I believe, however, that the saints are willing to pray, to rejoice, and to give thanks. Concerning rejoicing, we must practice, not rejoicing occasionally, but rejoicing always. The same is true regarding prayer. We should not pray just once in a while, but unceasingly. What breathing is to our physical life, prayer is to our spiritual life. Breathing is more necessary than eating, drinking, or sleeping. Praying must be first in our spiritual life. We must breathe by praying unceasingly. There is no need for us to be alone in our room in order to pray. While we are speaking, listening, or busy with other things, we can pray. In everything we do, we are able to breathe. Medical science has learned that breathing deeply is a great help to our health. Regarding our spiritual breathing, we should not pray in a shallow way, but pray from the depths of our being. When we pray like this, we stir up our spirit and fan the fire within us. Then we shall rejoice and give thanks to the Lord. If we do these three things, the indwelling Spirit within us will be burning. By this burning Spirit within, we shall be willing to remain in death and to keep the flesh, the self, and the natural life on the cross. This experience of death will usher in resurrection.

As we have pointed out, death is the gateway into resurrection. The deeper we go into death, the greater will be our experience of resurrection. When we have an outstanding death, we shall also have an outstanding resurrection. The way to have such an outstanding death is to rejoice always, to pray unceasingly, and to give thanks in everything. When we do these things, we are in Him and in His resurrection. In Philippians 3 Paul speaks of knowing Christ and the power of His resurrection. Here Christ equals the power of resurrection. When we are in Him, we are in the power of resurrection. In the power of resurrection we can do all things. This is the experience of Christ recorded in the book of Philippians. In chapter one Paul speaks of Christ being magnified in him, whether by death or by life, and in chapter four he says that he can do all things in the One who empowers him. The way to be in the empowering One is to rejoice, pray, and give thanks. If we do these things, the Spirit will work out the experience of death, and this death will bring us into resurrection. Eventually, we shall arrive at the outstanding resurrection from among the dead.